Practice Papers for SQA Exams

Higher

Physical Education

Questions and answers do not emanate from SQA. All of our entirely new and original Practice Papers have been written by experienced authors working directly for the publisher.

ISBN 978-1-84372-876-4

Published by
Leckie & Leckie Ltd
An imprint of HarperCollins*Publishers*
Westerhill Road, Bishopbriggs, Glasgow, G64 2QT
T: 0844 576 8126   F: 0844 576 8131
leckieandleckie@harpercollins.co.uk   www.leckieandleckie.co.uk

Special thanks to
Exemplarr (creative packaging)
Kate Manson (proofreader)
Roda Morrison (copy-editor)
Virginie Renard (proofreader)

A CIP Catalogue record for this book is available from the British Library.

Acknowledgements
Leckie & Leckie has made every effort to trace all copyright holders.
If any have been inadvertently overlooked, we will be pleased to make the necessary arrangements.

Introduction

Layout of the book

This book contains practice exam papers which mirror the actual SQA exam as much as possible. The layout and question level are all similar to the actual exam that you will sit, so that you become familiar with what the exam paper will look like.

The answer section is at the back of the book. Each answer uses activity-specific examples to illustrate the depth, detail and quality of information that should be included in your answers to get full marks. The answers also include practical tips on how to tackle certain types of questions, details of how marks are awarded and advice on just what the examiners will be looking for.

Revision advice is provided in this introductory section of the book, so please read on!

How to use this book

The practice papers can be used in two important ways:

1. You can complete an entire practice paper as preparation for the final exam. If you would like to use the book in this way, you can complete the practice paper under exam-style conditions by setting yourself a time for each paper and answering it as well as possible without using any references or notes. Alternatively, you can answer the practice paper questions as a revision exercise, using your notes to produce a model answer.

2. You can use the Topic Index at the front of this book to find all the questions within the book that deal with a specific topic. This allows you to focus specifically on areas that you particularly want to revise or, if you are mid-way through your course, it lets you practise answering exam-style questions for just those topics that you have studied.

Revision advice

Work out a revision timetable for each week's work in advance – remember to cover all of your subjects and to leave time for homework and breaks. For example:

Day	6pm–6.45pm	7pm–8pm	8.15pm–9pm	9.15pm–10pm
Monday	Homework	Homework	English revision	Chemistry revision
Tuesday	Maths revision	Physics revision	Homework	Free
Wednesday	PE Revision	Modern Studies revision	English revision	French revision
Thursday	Homework	Maths revision	Chemistry revision	Free
Friday	PE Revision	French revision	Free	Free
Saturday	Free	Free	Free	Free
Sunday	Modern Studies revision	Maths revision	Modern Studies revision	Homework

Make sure that you have at least one evening a week free to relax, socialise and re-charge your batteries. It also gives your brain a chance to process the information that you have been feeding it all week.

Arrange your study time into 1-hour or 30-minute sessions, with a break between sessions, e.g. 6pm–7pm, 7.15pm–7.45pm, 8pm–9pm. Try to start studying as early as possible in the evening when your brain is still alert and be aware that the longer you put off starting, the harder it will be to start!

Study a different subject in each session, except for the day before an exam.

Do something different during your breaks between study sessions – have a cup of tea or listen to some music. Don't let your 15 minutes expand into 20 or 25 minutes though!

Have your class notes and any textbooks available for your revision to hand, as well as plenty of blank paper, a pen, etc. You may like to make keyword sheets like the physical education example below:

Keyword	Meaning
Frequency	how often you do something
Concentration	the ability to focus on task related information
Continuous training	exercising without rest intervals

Finally, forget or ignore all or some of the advice in this section if you are happy with your present way of studying. Everyone revises differently, so find a way that works for you!

Transfer your knowledge

As you work through your class notes, textbooks and NABs to revise, these practice papers will also be a useful revision tool as they will help you to get used to answering exam-style questions. You may find, as you work through the questions, that they refer to a Key Concept or Key Feature(s) you have not studied before. Don't worry! Much will depend on the activities you have studied or been involved in. You should, however, be able to transfer your knowledge in relation to your personal performance focus and development. Personal reflection on how you analyse, train, practise and prepare for performance within activities will promote your understanding of the associated theoretical principles. The enhanced answer section at the back of the book will guide you on how to read and interpret the question asked, to ensure you demonstrate your knowledge and understanding of concepts and enable you to answer questions successfully.

Command words

The Physical Education exam paper is set in a structured manner with questions testing your understanding of both acquired and applied knowledge of the Analysis of Performance areas.

A number of command words will be used to guide you as to what knowledge is being targeted by the question.

In these practice papers you will work with these command words to increase your confidence at interpreting what is being asked of you and help you to structure your answers more effectively.

Command words	Response required
Describe Describe in detail	Give the facts about the subject of the question. Without interpreting the information: • give information • convey a mental picture • give an account.
Outline	Brief identification of a point, with a little explanation. Offer the main points.
Identify	Pick out some of the key factors. List or name them. Demonstrate how factors are related.
Analyse	Examine closely. Look at the facts/evidence/data and interpret what you find. Qualify and/or quantify facts.
Explain Explain in detail	May require definition or description. Determine the value of something. Identify criteria by which something will be measured. THINK about the HOW and WHY. Give reasons.
Suggest	Make a judgement and give examples to support your answer. Decide the value of.

Compare	Point out similarities and differences between one or more factors.
Discuss/justify	Examine closely, taking account of strengths and weaknesses. Argue for and against, criticise/appraise in terms of impact on/ significance to performance development. Offer reasons. Refer to evidence/data. Substantiate your opinion.
Evaluate/assess	Make judgements, look at the evidence and back up points raised. Substantiate your opinion.

TOP EXAM TIP

If you can grasp the precise wording of the questions and the precise meanings of the command words, you will be able to answer the question clearly. BE CONFIDENT!

In the exam

- **Before** you start writing, **read** the **whole** question paper first. Read questions right through before you choose to attempt them; perhaps the second part of the question asks for something you do not know about and so you would be better to select a different question.

- Select the three questions that you know most about (refer to all parts (a), (b), (c) and (d)). While you may be able to tailor what you know to answer a given question, it is important to resist the temptation to answer the question you hoped would be asked, or to write down everything you know that is vaguely related to the question.

- Plan the order you will answer the questions in. For example, it may be a good idea to start by re-using the analysis answer from your NAB to answer one of the questions.

- Underline or highlight the command words and important phrases.

- Be aware of your write-up time for each of the three questions – share out your time effectively!

- Try to leave some time at the end of the exam so that you can check over your answers. A little time spent checking can sometimes save you quite a lot of marks and could make the difference between an A, B or C grade.

TOP EXAM TIP

Exam practice and revision are the keys to success. Remember, everyone revises differently, so find a way that works for you.

Topic Index

Topic	Exam A	Exam B	Exam C	Knowledge for Prelim			Knowledge for SQA Exam		
				Have difficulty	Still needs work	OK	Have difficulty	Still needs work	OK
Performance Appreciation	1(a), 1(b), 1(c), 1(d), 2(a), 2(b), 2(c), 2(d)	1(a), 1(b), 1(c), 1(d), 2(a), 2(b), 2(c), 2(d)	1(a), 1(b), 1(c), 1(d), 2(a), 2(b), 2(c)(i), 2(c)(ii), 2(d)						
Preparation of the Body	3(a), 3(b), 3(c), 3(d), 4(a), 4(b), 4(c), 4(d)	3(a), 3(b), 3(c), 3(d), 4(a), 4(b), 4(c), 4(d)	3(a), 3(b), 3(c), 3(d), 4(a), 4(b), 4(c), 4(d)						
Skills and Techniques	5(a), 5(b), 5(c), 5(d), 6(a), 6(b), 6(c), 6(d)	5(a), 5(b), 5(c), 5(d), 6(a), 6(b), 6(c), 6(d)	5(a), 5(b), 5(c), 5(d), 6(a), 6(b), 6(c), 6(d)						
Structures and Strategies	7(a), 7(b), 7(c), 7(d), 8(a), 8(b), 8(c), 8(d)	7(a), 7(b)(i), 7(b)(ii), 7(c), 7(d), 8(a), 8(b), 8(c), 8(d)	7(a), 7(b), 7(c), 7(d), 8(a), 8(b), 8(c), 8(d)						

Physical Education | Analysis and Development of Performance

Practice Papers	Higher Level
For SQA Exams	Examination
Examination A	

Candidate instructions

You are allowed 2 hours and 30 minutes to complete this paper.

You must complete **three questions**, each chosen from a different area.

Questions should be read carefully before answering.

A total of 60 marks is available in this examination.

Leckie x Leckie
Scotland's leading educational publishers

AREA 1: PERFORMANCE APPRECIATION

Marks

Question 1

Choose an activity.

(a) Describe the demands of a **quality** performance within your chosen activity.

4

(b) Compared to a model performer, discuss the differences in your performance.

6

(c) Discuss how you improved your performance to more closely match that of a model performer.

6

(d) Performance can be influenced by mental factors such as:

- **Managing emotions**
- **Mental preparation**
- **Mental state.**

Explain, in detail, how **one** of these factors has influenced your performance.

4

(20)

Question 2

Select an activity.

(a) Describe the nature of this activity. Also describe the demands of this activity.

6

(b) Mental factors affect the way you perform.

Explain how mental factors can affect your performance and the methods you have used to manage these.

4

(c) Discuss why it can be important to use integrated (combination) training to develop your whole performance.

6

(d) It is best to both monitor and review your performance development. Why?

4

(20)

AREA 2: PREPARATION OF THE BODY

Marks

Question 3

Choose an activity.

(a) Describe, in detail, the range of fitness requirements for your selected activity.

6

(b) Explain what you would take into account when planning a training programme.

4

(c) There are three phases or periods of training:

- preparation (pre-season)
- competition (during the season)
- transition (off season).

Select **two** of these phases and describe, in detail, the content of the training programme you carried out in each phase.

6

(d) Explain why it is important to evaluate the effectiveness of your training programme.

4

(20)

Question 4

Choose an activity.

(a) Select a skill-related aspect of fitness. Describe how you gathered information on this aspect of fitness.

4

(b) Why is mental fitness important in your activity?

4

(c) Training can take place:

- within the activity (conditioning)
- outwith the activity
- through a combination of both.

Select **one** of the above and briefly describe a training programme. Explain why this training approach is appropriate.

6

(d) During training you may have made changes to your programme. Discuss why these changes were necessary. Give examples to support your answer.

6

(20)

AREA 3: SKILLS AND TECHNIQUES

Marks

Question 5

(a) Explain what you understand about information processing.   **4**

(b) When developing a skill or technique, explain the practice method(s) you used to improve your performance.   **6**

(c) Describe how you monitored your improvement during your practice.   **4**

(d) When developing this skill or technique, explain why feedback and motivation were important.   **6**

    (20)

Question 6

Choose an activity.

(a) Explain what you understand about the stages of learning, with reference to the activity you have chosen.   **6**

(b) With reference to a stage of your learning, describe your performance of a skill or technique.   **4**

(c) Describe the principles you applied when practising to improve the skill or technique you identified in part (b).   **6**

(d) Why is it important to review your skill or technique development?   **4**

    (20)

AREA 4: STRUCTURES, STRATEGIES AND COMPOSITION

Marks

Question 7

Choose an activity.

(*a*) Describe, in detail, a structure, strategy or composition you have used.

4

(*b*) What factors did you take into consideration before selecting this structure, strategy or composition? Give examples to support your answer.

6

(*c*) Briefly describe a situation where you had to **adapt** or **change** your structure, strategy or composition. Explain why these changes or adaptations made your performance more effective.

6

(*d*) Describe how you evaluated your changes or adaptations to see if they had been successful.

4

(20)

Question 8

(*a*) Describe a structure, strategy or composition you have used in an **individual** activity of your choice.

4

(*b*) Describe how you collected data on your performance when applying this structure, strategy or composition. Why were the methods you used appropriate?

4

(*c*) Briefly describe the weaknesses you found in the structure, strategy or composition from the data collected. Discuss the course of action you took to address these weaknesses.

6

(*d*) Structures, strategies and compositions are based on certain key principles/ fundamentals. Select **two** that you have used and explain their importance when applying your structure, strategy or composition.

6

(20)

[END OF QUESTION PAPER]

Physical Education | Analysis and Development of Performance

Practice Papers
For SQA Exams
Examination B

Higher Level
Examination

Candidate instructions

You are allowed 2 hours and 30 minutes to complete this paper.

You must complete **three questions**, each chosen from a different area.

Questions should be read carefully before answering.

A total of 60 marks is available in this examination.

Scotland's leading educational publishers

AREA 1: PERFORMANCE APPRECIATION

Marks

Question 1

(a) Why is goal setting important for your performance improvement? **4**

Choose an activity.

(b) Outline the methods you used to collect data on your performance in an activity. Explain what your analysis of the data showed. **6**

(c) In relation to your data analysis, describe, in detail, a training programme you used to develop your performance. **6**

(d) Explain how your performance was affected on completion of your training. **4**

(20)

Question 2

Choose an activity.

(a) Explain why it can be easier to perform during training/practice sessions than in competitive situations. **4**

(b) Describe, in detail, how you gathered information on your performance either during training sessions or in the competitive performance situation. Why is this important? **6**

(c) With reference to a specific competitive performance, describe what you did to try to ensure you performed to the best of your ability. **6**

(d) For future performance development, outline (a) performance goal(s) you would set. Briefly describe how you would achieve this (these). **4**

(20)

AREA 2: PREPARATION OF THE BODY   *Marks*

Question 3

(*a*) Select an aspect of fitness important to your activity and describe how you gathered information on this aspect of fitness both **within** and **outwith** your activity.   **6**

(*b*) Explain why it is important to collect information on your fitness before planning a training programme.   **4**

(*c*) Discuss how you applied the principles of training when planning a programme to improve the aspect of fitness selected in part (*a*).   **6**

(*d*) Discuss the effects that your training had on your performance.   **4**

                                                                              (20)

Question 4

Choose an activity.

(*a*) Physical, skill-related and mental fitness are important for effective performance within your activity. Select **one** aspect of **each type** of fitness and explain its importance for effective performance.   **6**

(*b*) Select **one** aspect of fitness from part (*a*). Describe one method of training you used to develop this aspect of fitness.   **4**

(*c*) Explain why this method of training was appropriate.   **4**

(*d*) Discuss the importance of setting goals to improve your level of fitness. Give examples of goals you have set.   **6**

                                                                              (20)

AREA 3: SKILLS AND TECHNIQUES

Marks

Question 5

Choose an activity.

(*a*) Describe **two** methods you used to gather information on your performance of skills or techniques.

4

(*b*) From your analysis of this information, describe your skill development needs.

4

(*c*) Discuss the practice programme you used to improve your skill development.

6

(*d*) Discuss the effect of your practice methods on your whole performance. Why may there still be (a) weakness(es) in your performance?

6

(20)

Question 6

Choose an activity.

(*a*) Give a detailed description of a complex skill, outlining what makes it difficult to perform.

4

(*b*) Describe, in detail, the method(s) of practice you used to develop this complex skill.

6

(*c*) Discuss the principles you considered to ensure your practice was effective. Give examples of how these were used within your sessions.

6

(*d*) What are the benefits of using a model performer to help you to perform this complex skill?

4

(20)

AREA 4: STRUCTURES, STRATEGIES AND COMPOSITION   *Marks*

Question 7

Choose an activity.

(*a*) Describe a structure, strategy or composition you have used in this activity. Briefly outline the role you played.   **6**

(*b*) Explain the benefits that can be gained when applying your chosen structure, strategy or composition.   **4**

(*c*) (i) Explain **one** limitation that has to be taken into account when applying this structure, strategy or composition.   **2**

(ii) Explain what you would do to overcome this limitation.   **2**

(*d*) Discuss some of the decisions you faced when performing in this structure, strategy or composition to ensure you carried out your role effectively.   **6**

    (20)

Question 8

Choose an activity and a structure, strategy or composition.

(*a*) Discuss why it is important to gather information on your performance when applying the structure, strategy or composition. Outline the strengths and weaknesses you found from the information gathered.   **6**

(*b*) Describe the course of action you took to improve the weaknesses you identified in part (*a*).   **4**

(*c*) Having carried out a course of action to improve your weaknesses, how did you monitor the effectiveness of your training programme? Briefly outline what would be your future development needs having carried out your programme.   **6**

(*d*) Why is the monitoring process important?   **4**

    (20)

[END OF QUESTION PAPER]

Physical Education | Analysis and Development of Performance

Practice Papers
For SQA Exams
Examination C

Higher Level
Examination

Candidate instructions

You are allowed 2 hours and 30 minutes to complete this paper.

You must complete **three questions**, each chosen from a different area.

Questions should be read carefully before answering.

A total of 60 marks is available in this examination.

Scotland's leading educational publishers

AREA 1: PERFORMANCE APPRECIATION

Marks

Question 1

Choose an activity.

(a) When preparing for a **quality** performance, describe the various factors you took into account.

4

(b) Explain how you planned your performance development to ensure you were ready to produce your best possible **quality** performance.

6

(c) Discuss how individual differences can affect the outcome of a performance.

Outline a performance situation where your individual characteristics affected the outcome.

6

(d) How did you gather information on the performance outlined in part (c)?

4

(20)

Question 2

(a) Explain the different ways model performers may be helpful in developing your performance in an activity.

4

Choose an activity.

(b) From your performance, discuss how you use your strengths to best effect. Outline a significant weakness which affects your performance.

6

(c) Discuss how you would plan your training to
(i) improve your weakness

OR

(ii) maintain or further develop your strengths.

6

(d) Discuss how you monitored your performance during your training.

4

(20)

AREA 2: PREPARATION OF THE BODY

Marks

Question 3

(a)
- Physical fitness
- Skill-related fitness
- Mental fitness

Select **two** of the three types of fitness above and explain the importance of these two types when performing in an **individual** activity.   **6**

(b)
- Physical fitness
- Skill-related fitness
- Mental fitness

From the three types of fitness above, select the **remaining** type of fitness, not chosen in part (a), and explain the importance of this type when performing in a **team** activity.   **4**

(c) Select **one** of the types of fitness from part (a) or part (b). Discuss what you took into account when you planned a fitness training programme for this type of fitness. Give examples from your programme to support your answer.   **6**

(d) Describe **one** method you used to monitor the effectiveness of your training programme. Explain why this method was appropriate.   **4**

(20)

Question 4

(a) Select **two** different activities. Describe two physical fitness requirements that are similar in both activities. Give examples to support your answer.   **4**

(b) Select **one** of the activities described in part (a) and explain why skill-related fitness is important when performing.   **4**

(c) From the **other** activity selected in part (a), discuss why mental fitness is important. Give examples to support your answer.   **6**

(d) Select **one** of the aspects of fitness from your answers above. Select one method of training you used to develop this aspect. Explain why this method was appropriate. Describe, in detail, **one** training session using this method.   **6**

(20)

AREA 3: SKILLS AND TECHNIQUES

Marks

Question 5

(a) From an activity of your choice, outline some of the features of performance that can be identified at each of the stages of skill learning. Explain what you understand about each stage.

6

(b) Select a skill or technique from your activity. Give a detailed analysis of your performance that shows your current stage of learning.

4

(c) When developing this skill or technique, discuss how you used your knowledge of skill learning to design an appropriate programme of work.

6

(d) Describe how you evaluated the effectiveness of the programme you used.

4

(20)

Question 6

Choose an activity and a skill or technique.

(a) Describe how you gathered information on your performance in the selected skill or technique.

4

(b) Describe, in detail, a practice programme you used to develop this skill or technique.

6

(c) Outline what you understand about the following **three factors** when practising or refining skills and/or techniques.

- **Motivation**
- **Concentration**
- **Feedback**

6

(d) Explain why it is important to monitor and review the effectiveness of your practice programme.

4

(20)

AREA 4: STRUCTURES, STRATEGIES AND COMPOSITION

Marks

Question 7

Choose an activity and a structure, strategy or composition.

(a) Discuss the strengths that players need to carry out this structure, strategy or composition effectively.

4

(b) Describe the problem(s) you faced when carrying out this structure, strategy or composition. Explain the effect it had on your performance.

6

(c) Describe in detail the programme of work you carried out to address the problems identified in part (b).

6

(d) Describe **one** method you used to see if your programme of work was effective. Explain why this method was appropriate.

4

(20)

Question 8

Choose an activity.

(a) Describe a structure, strategy or composition you would usually select as your first choice. Explain why you would choose to use this structure, strategy or composition.

6

(b) Describe an alternative structure, strategy or composition you might use in your chosen activity.

4

(c) Choose **one** of the factors listed below:

- dealing with pressure
- being creative
- exercising effective solutions
- being perceptive.

Discuss how an awareness of this factor helped you to make decisions when applying your structure, strategy or composition selected in part (a).

6

(d) Describe how you would evaluate the effectiveness of your structure, strategy or composition in relation to the factor selected in part (c).

4

(20)

[END OF QUESTION PAPER]

Answers

PERFORMANCE APPRECIATION

Question 1

Choose an activity.

(a) Describe the demands of a quality performance within your chosen activity. **4**

TOP EXAM TIP

Knowing what each command word means will help you to answer fully and pick up available marks. For an explanation of command words, see pages 4–5.

HINT The question is asking for your knowledge & the specific demands that you will face when performing in your activity. By outlining the technical, physical, mental and tactical demands you will be exhibiting your depth of understanding.

TOP EXAM TIP

Remember – exams are designed to reward your preparation and study work. Relax and just simply recall what you know.

I play setter for my school volleyball team. There are many different demands of a quality performance in my role. Firstly, the technical demands of both attacking and defending. The skills required are setting, digging, spiking, blocking, serving and court coverage. These are needed to keep the rallies going and set up winning opportunities.

(1 mark)

There are physical demands such as cardio-respiratory endurance to last for the full game and speed endurance to cope with tiring rallies. Speed is needed to cover the court quickly. Power and muscular endurance are needed to repeatedly jump to spike or block at the net.

(1 mark)

The game is mentally demanding and I need to remain focused and concentrate on all shots played so that I do not let my team down. I need to be alert and work co-operatively with my team as the game tempo can change quickly, requiring me to attack one minute and move back to cover in defence the next. (1 mark)

I also need to be aware of the tactical demands of the game, for example I need to be aware of my team strategy so that I play my role (setter) well. I must also have the ability to recognise my opponents' strategies so that I can set the ball well off the net for my hitters and get into good cover positions, jumping to block or falling back to cover the dump ball. (1 mark)

(b) Compared to a model performer, discuss the differences in your performance. **6**

TOP EXAM TIP

Offering a synopsis of your strengths and weaknesses will help you identity the main differences.

HINT This question demands analytical thinking. Comparing your technical, physical and mental strengths and weaknesses will enable you to access full marks.

When compared to the model performer, I feel I have a wide range of technical skills, although my skills are not as accurate. I can set well to allow my spikers a good attacking option. My defending in block situations is good as I make correct decisions regarding when to jump or crouch down to cover the dump. (1 mark)

Like the model performer, I have high levels of physical fitness to enable me to perform my role. I am fast, agile and have a good range of flexibility. This is important when having to dive and pick up shots or when using reverse volleys. (1 mark) I have good cardio-respiratory endurance which helps me cope with long rallies. (1 mark)

Unlike the model performer, I can at times lack speed off the mark. This can put us under pressure, as I fail to get to wide balls that are hit out of court. Quicker chasing would keep the ball in play. (1 mark)

I am not as mentally controlled as the model performer. I can be very competitive and in tight matches the pressure can upset my timing and rhythm of playing shots. I sometimes overset which limits our attack.(1 mark)

I pride myself on always showing respect for my opponents. I like to be considered a fair player and good loser. I would like to demonstrate more special qualities in my game and show more flair and creativity in my play. (1 mark)

(c)   Discuss how you improved your performance to more closely match that of a model performer.   **6**

TOP EXAM TIP

In this analysis area you can select fitness training or skill development programmes used to improve your overall performance, or a combination of both.

HINT   Remember, a discussion relies on your critical thinking skills. This means you should offer examples and justify your decisions. Note how the use of diagrams can support your answer.

Firstly, I watched the model performer and set myself targets. My long term targets were to develop my ability as a setter by remaining calm and focusing on improving the timing of my shots and also my speed off the mark to chase balls going out of court. (1 mark) My immediate target was to plan a skills programme specifically aimed at addressing these weaknesses. I considered training options and knew that a programme based on appropriate drills for my role and stage of learning would work best. (1 mark) At practice sessions, I did a series of reaction, pressure and combination drills. During these rallies I visualised in my head how a model performer would play the shot. This helped me to focus on my actions. (1 mark)

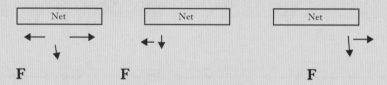

In each of these three drills, the feeder threw the ball wide for me so that I ran in specific directions to chase the ball and play it back into court. The shot I practised was my dig. I did this six times and got feedback from the feeder. (1 mark)

To progress, my feeder played ten random feeds. This time my target was to play either a set or dig high enough for the spiker to attack at the net. This put me under pressure. (1 mark)

I then played combination rallies of serve–dig–set–spike before finishing with small-sided games. This allowed me to react to where the ball and my teammates were. As my programme was specific, and I could make drills harder as I became more successful, my performance moved more towards a model performance. (1 mark)

(d)   Performance can be influenced by mental factors such as:

•   **Managing emotions**

•   **Mental preparation**

•   **Mental state.**

Explain, in detail, how **one** of these factors has influenced your performance.   4

TOP EXAM TIP

Make sure you select the factor you know most about.

HINT This question prompts you to be reflective about your own performance experiences – convince the examiner of this by offering personal examples. Remember, depending on your own personal qualities you may have both positive and negative experiences.

I have been in situations where my mental state has had a negative effect on my performance. Before playing an important final I suffered from cognitive anxiety. The thought of facing our rivals worried me. Deep down, I knew we could beat them, but I feared that, if we got off to bad start, we would struggle to come back from behind. (1 mark) During close rallies, I have also suffered from somatic anxiety. This nervousness upsets my rhythm and timing when placing my shots. My heart rate quickens and I tend to rush shots as a result. I often overset for my spikers and our opponents capitalise on this. (1 mark) When in this poor state of arousal I feel I lose confidence and definitely make more unforced errors. Unfortunately, I show this lack of confidence in my body language and my teammates can sometimes become demoralised. (1 mark)

Ideally, I would always like to have a positive mental state both before and during performance as this would enable me to control my emotions, deal with pressure situations, and help me to be more fluent in my passing options. (1 mark)

Question 2

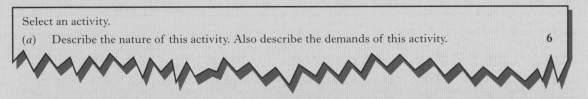

Select an activity.

(a)   Describe the nature of this activity. Also describe the demands of this activity.   6

TOP EXAM TIP

Be methodical by writing down the headings of 'nature' and 'demands' and offering examples to support your answer. Always be aware of the mark allocation.

HINT Note the 6 mark allocation. Giving equal detail about the nature and demands will ensure you access full marks. This question requires logical thinking. Imagine the reader knows nothing about your activity; your account should inform and expand their appreciation.

Hockey is fast and exciting. It is a directly competitive game with two teams of 11v11, plus subs to roll on in the event of injury or a change of tactics. The object of the game is to score more goals than the other team. (1 mark) The game lasts 70 minutes with 35 minutes each half. There are a number of rules to make sure players play fairly. All players need to play as hard as they can and accept the decision of the referee if they commit a foul. (1 mark) Good conduct and discipline are expected. The game is played outdoors and so the weather and state of competition may affect the players and the end result. (1 mark)

The demands of hockey are really challenging. All players have attacking and defending duties and this puts pressure on the players to perform well. There are physical, technical and tactical demands. Here is an example of each.

There are many physical demands. Players need high levels of muscular endurance and speed endurance to enable them to sprint into position to receive/intercept passes or track back to deny their opponents space and time on the ball. They must also last for the duration of the 70 minute game. (1 mark)

The technical level of dribbling, passing, shooting and tackling, etc., must be of a high and consistent standard to expose opponents' weaknesses. Players need to respond to these demands by constantly applying their skills with split-second timing. (1 mark)

The tactical demands are challenging, with players having to co-operate and respond to the immediate game problem. In any given situation, tactics will be used to gain the benefits of width and depth and so control the tempo of the game. It is important that players know when to switch and adapt play to gain territorial advantage. (1 mark)

(b)   Mental factors affect the way you perform.

Explain how mental factors can affect your performance and the methods you have used to manage these.   4

HINT Note how the statement stimulates your opinion. The question requires you to show your knowledge about mental factors but, more importantly, it requires you to emphasise the method(s) you have used to manage your emotions.

I know that mental factors can have either a positive or negative effect on performance.

My mental state is affected by somatic anxiety which, if I let it, would have a negative effect on my performance. When playing in important matches, I get uptight and suffer from the obvious symptoms of sweaty palms, butterflies in stomach, etc. (1 mark) My coach has taught me about breathing and visualisation techniques. The beauty of these techniques is that they can be used before and during the game and performed very quickly.   (1 mark)

I have learned about better preparation; for example, in the changing rooms, when I feel my breathing getting faster and my stomach jittery, I visualise myself dribbling under control and shooting into the low corners of goal. This slows my breathing down.   (1 mark)

During the game, in tough tackles or if we are having to come from behind, I get anxious and my concentration drifts. When this happens, I take a deep breath and count to five and then from five back down again; this rebuilds my confidence and can help me think a bit more clearly.   (1 mark)

(c)   Discuss why it can be important to use integrated (combination) training to develop your whole performance.   6

HINT   The question challenges your understanding of: (i) integrated training and (ii) developing your whole performance. Remember – when asked to discuss, you need to be able to justify and back up your opinion.

Using integrated training helps me to deal with two or more parts of my performance at the same time.

This saves time and often makes it more enjoyable; for example, it is much more fun doing repetition dribbling drills at speed than doing dribbling practice and then going for a series of shuttle runs.   (1 mark)

My skills and fitness can be developed more in game-like situations. For example, sometimes the drills can be performed in isolation and then with the added pressure of competing against defenders.   (1 mark)

The nature of hockey relies on team effort and so practising with your team mates builds up co-operation and tactical awareness.   (1 mark)

It provides excellent competitive challenge between teammates. For example, when practising technical skills, such as passing in twos, a set target of first pair to reach fifteen wins a point. This develops control, accuracy and speed of passing.   (1 mark)

Game-related set pieces, such as taking corners or free hits, can help to develop other qualities such as my timing, movement and anticipation of when to move, cut into space, deny my opponents and support play.
                                                                        (1 mark)

Work rate can be easily planned and adapted, i.e. work continuously with little rest periods, or put more focus on particular aspects of physical, technical or tactical fitness as appropriate, to improve specific weaknesses. This can make me better prepared for the whole game.   (1 mark)

TOP EXAM TIP

Convince the examiner you can justify your opinion by giving specific examples of what can be involved in integrated training. Remember – examples will be wide-ranging, according to your performance focus.

(d)   It is best to both monitor and review your performance development. Why?   4

HINT   The question challenges your understanding of the processes of monitoring and reviewing. In the examples you give make sure you explain the differences. Note the 2 mark allocation split.

TOP EXAM TIP

Giving two examples from each process will ensure you access full marks.

I know that it is very important to do both. Monitoring should be done all the time and is important because it tells me how my performance is changing and progressing. Reviewing should be done at the end of my training and tells me if I have been successful in reaching my performance targets.   (1 mark)

For example, during my training I always monitored how I was doing as this kept me motivated and provided me with immediate feedback: my coach would tell me why I had not performed a specific part of my passing technique well. I could then practise based on what I was told. (1 mark)

Monitoring is done all the time, mainly from internal feedback. I know if my short term targets are being reached and this helps me to focus on the things I still need to improve upon. (1 mark)

Reviewing helps when my training is complete. It lets me compare early performances to my most current. I am able to check whether the training has worked. (1 mark)

OR

Reviewing my performance training lets me judge whether or not to continue training on the same aspects or whether to move on and address other weaknesses in my performance. (1 mark)

Worked answers to Practice Paper A, Area 2

PREPARATION OF THE BODY

> **TOP EXAM TIP**
>
> Read over both questions in Area 2 before deciding which one to answer. You don't have enough time to start a question and then decide you can't answer it.

Question 3

> Choose an activity.
>
> (a) Describe, in detail, the range of fitness requirements for your selected activity. **6**

The activity I have chosen is swimming. My main event is the 100 metres freestyle. CRE is the body's ability to work for long periods of time without becoming tired. It is important that I have a high level of CRE so I can work harder for longer and be able to maintain my technique and breathing for as long as possible before I get tired. (1 mark)

Strength is also important in swimming, as I am working the muscles of the arm and shoulder to generate propulsion to pull my body through the water. The stronger my arm pulls, the more effective my stroke will become. (1 mark)

Skill-related fitness is also required in swimming in regard to the need for good co-ordination. Co-ordination is the body's ability to work different parts at the same time. Working arms and legs together helps me produce the most efficient and effective stroke. For example, in front crawl, as one arm is pulling, the opposite leg should be kicking downwards. (1 mark)

Reaction time is also required at the start of a race. As soon as the gun or hooter sounds, I want to react quickly and push off the blocks to enter the water quickly and efficiently. (1 mark)

Finally, I also require mental fitness. I need to manage my emotions when I am competing. I must focus on what I am doing, be positive throughout the event and not let myself become anxious or distracted. (1 mark) I also need good concentration so I can maintain good technique in my stroke and ensure I can achieve an effective tumble turn at the end of each length. (1 mark)

> **HINT** Remember, your activity may have different fitness requirements. Make the link to the specific fitness demands of your role or activity requirements which will help you demonstrate your knowledge of fitness.

> (b) Explain what you would take into account when planning a training programme. **4**

When planning a training programme, it is important to make sure that the training is specific to the individual as well as the activity. It is therefore important to have knowledge of the fitness demands of the activity and then to find out my level of fitness prior to starting the programme. This will ensure that the training programme is relevant and leads not only to an improvement in fitness but also an improvement in my performance. (1 mark)

It is also important for the training programme to have a particular aim so I can set myself both short term and long term goals. This will motivate me to train hard. Without goals I will have no aim to work towards and I will become less interested and motivated when training and would improve less. (1 mark)

I also need to make sure the training programme takes into account the principles of training. I need to consider how often (frequency) and how long (duration) I will train for. I have decided to train for six to eight weeks, three times per week, for at least 30 minutes per session. I will also ensure that during my programme I apply the principle of overload. (1 mark)

Finally, I also need to take into account the type of training that I would do to improve my fitness. As I am trying to improve my CRE, I will use interval training. This will allow me to work using high intensity swimming alternating with periods of rest. I will also carry out this training in the swimming pool. (1 mark)

TOP EXAM TIP

Knowing what each command word means is crucial in being able to answer questions correctly and pick up marks. For an explanation of command words, see pages 4–5.

HINT Think about your own personal training. At your planning stage, what did you take into account? This will help you answer in depth and detail.

(c)   There are three phases or periods of training:

- preparation (pre-season)
- competition (during the season)
- transition (off season).

Select **two** of these phases and describe, in detail, the content of the training programme you carried out in each phase.   **6**

TOP EXAM TIP

Descriptions need details, not just the basic points. Using examples strengthens your answer.

I am going to select the preparation phase and the competition phase. In the preparation phase, I was trying to build up general fitness and in particular my aerobic endurance. I did this by running long/slow distance runs twice per week to start with. Each run lasted 20/30 minutes. As I got nearer to the competition phase, I gradually increased the intensity of the programme by increasing the amount of time I was running to 40/50 minutes. (1 mark)

I also devised a circuit which was a group of particular exercises to build up my level of muscular endurance and CRE. I had six stations where I did exercises such as press ups, sit ups, burpees, stride jumps, step ups and shuttle runs. I did 30 seconds of each exercise and then moved on. I completed three circuits. Again, I increased the intensity as I got fitter. (1 mark)

I also trained in the swimming pool to improve my CRE. I did interval training. I started with a warm up of four lengths. My main set was 6 × 50 metres swim with a minute rest after each set. I used a heart monitor to make sure I was training within my training zone. I finished with a warm down in each session. (1 mark)

In the competition phase, I spent more time working in the pool. I concentrated on fine tuning my timing and co-ordination which are important for my arm pull and leg kick. I also spent time improving my tumble turn approach which should lead to an improvement in my co-ordination and hopefully to a better and more efficient turn. (1 mark)

Outwith the pool, I worked twice per week on improving specific aspects of fitness specifically for my event, such as strength. This took the form of a weights circuit where I would lift heavy weights with low repetitions. The exercises included bench press, arm curls, shoulder press and squats. I did three circuits of six reps working at 70/80% of my maximum weight. (1 mark)

Finally, it was important that I continued to maintain my level of fitness. I continued to do interval training as before, but I cut the recovery between each set to 45 seconds. I also made sure that, when I was approaching a peak performance for a race, my training was tapered down by decreasing the frequency and duration of each part of my training. (1 mark)

HINT It is important that you describe both stages in order to access full marks. If you only describe one stage you can only access half marks.

(d)   Explain why it is important to evaluate the effectiveness of your training programme.   **4**

TOP EXAM TIP

To explain means give reasons why a particular outcome has been reached or an action has been taken.

It is important to evaluate the effectiveness of my training programme to see if I achieved the goals that I had set beforehand. My goal was to improve my 100 metres time, which I did. This gave me the motivation to improve further.   (1 mark)

I compared my performance after training to my performance before training started. This enabled me to see if I had improved and determined what I still needed to work on in the future. I found I could still improve my reaction time to the 'go' command at the start of the event.   (1 mark)

I also checked whether the method of training had been suitable for me and whether the content of the programme was appropriate, so that improvement could be made in the weakness which I had identified previously.   (1 mark)

Finally, I wanted to make sure that the training had been effective and had been set at the correct intensity. There is no point in making the training too easy or improvement will be limited. If the training is set too hard, then you will struggle to carry it out and become demotivated.   (1 mark)

HINT   There are many different reasons for evaluating. Make sure you illustrate the purpose/benefits by giving specific examples.

Question 4

Choose an activity.

(a)   Select a skill-related aspect of fitness. Describe how you gathered information on this aspect of fitness.   **4**

HINT   The question is asking for a description of how you gathered information. Try to do it in such a way that the marker can easily picture how you did this.

TOP EXAM TIP

Think of other subjects where you are required to describe, e.g. in English. The command words mean the same thing.

I have chosen basketball. The aspect of skill-related fitness that I have chosen is agility as it is important in my role as guard. I gathered information on agility by doing the Illinois Agility test. I placed a set of cones as laid out in the diagram and I ran round this set course as fast as possible.   (1 mark)

I started by lying face down on the floor with my head to the start line and with hands by my shoulders. My partner then shouted 'go' and I had to get up and run as fast as possible round the course, as shown by the arrows in the diagram, without knocking any cones over.   (1 mark)

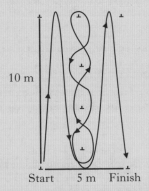

10 m

Start   5 m   Finish

I had to run round some cones and in and out of others and then run as fast as possible to the finish line.   (1 mark)

My partner took my time from start to finish using a stopwatch. I did three attempts and took an average of the three times. I then compared my times against national norms for my age.   (1 mark)

(b)   Why is mental fitness important in your activity?   **4**

> **HINT**   This question is asking you to think specifically about mental demands. Giving examples from your own performance will enhance your answer.

Basketball is a fast team game where contact happens and fouls occur, either committed by you or by someone against you. In a game, I am only allowed five fouls, after which I can take no further part. It is essential that I am able to control my emotions if I commit a foul in a game, or if I get upset if the referee gives a decision against me and I don't agree. If I don't, I may end up being fouled out or get frustrated, leading to mistakes.   (1 mark)

As my role is guard and I am the main playmaker in the team, I rehearse in my mind beforehand the plays that I will set up. For example, if my team play fast break I know that I need to get free to receive the first pass and then drive up the middle to pass the ball. Before the game starts my coach will go over all the plays.   (1 mark)

I also need to remain focused and calm during a game. When I am taking free throws, I need to block out all distractions such as the crowd or other players and fully concentrate on the technique and shot I am going to take. If I can do this there is more chance of success. Every point could be crucial.   (1 mark)

Confidence is important, as I want to carry out my role successfully. If I am not confident, I will make mistakes, such as poor passing or losing the ball, which will affect not only my performance but that of my team as well. I will become anxious and tense, leading to a poorer performance on my part.   (1 mark)

(c)   Training can take place:
- within the activity (conditioning)
- outwith the activity
- through a combination of both.

Select **one** of the above and briefly describe a training programme. Explain why this training approach is appropriate.   **6**

> **HINT**   This question is asking you to show acquired and applied knowledge about a training approach. Think back to your training. This will help you to answer this question in depth and detail.

I did a combination of both for basketball. I did a variety of practices involving skills and fitness. I practised my dribbling skills by setting up a course involving cones and I had to dribble in and out of them as fast as possible. I also made sure that I dribbled with different hands so I was becoming confident dribbling with either hand. I also did other exercises which improved my passing and shooting.   (1 mark)

I also did some Fartlek training outwith the activity, where I did different speeds of running with some short sprints as well as some continuous running. I varied the distances as well as the times.   (1 mark)

This approach was appropriate as I was able to work on the skills for the game, such as dribbling, and also, when improving my dribbling by going in and out of cones, I was working on improving my agility, which is important in my role as the playmaker.   (1 mark)

By working outwith the activity, I was able to work on specific aspects of fitness that are important for the activity such as CRE and speed.   (1 mark)

By working both within and outwith the activity, I could use different methods of training which gave me variety and prevented me from getting bored with the training. This kept me motivated and interested when training.   (1 mark)

Finally, the training allowed me to practise specific movements that are similar to game situations. For example, I was able to change direction when dribbling and also dribble at speed. This would be like me dribbling past opponents when trying to play the fast break.   (1 mark)

(d)   During training you may have made changes to your programme. Discuss why these
changes were necessary. Give examples to support your answer.   6

HINT   Reflect on your training and think of how you felt. Why did you change your training and what
did you do? By recalling this information you will find it easier to answer this question.

Changes were made to my programme because the training was no longer demanding enough for me and I had reached a plateau. I needed to make the training harder in order for me to continue progressing. If I had not made changes my performance would have stayed at the same level.   (1 mark)

I decided to train harder outwith the activity by increasing the time I trained from 30 to 45 minutes per session. This increased the distance I ran. It also improved my CRE fitness level by making the session more demanding.   (1 mark)

It also helped me to achieve my short term goal of improving my dribbling, as I felt much more comfortable when dribbling with my left hand, which had been my weak point previously when playing. I lost the ball less often and made fewer mistakes, making me contribute more in the games.   (1 mark)

I was becoming bored with training and I wanted to make progress in my performance. When I was bored I was not motivated to do better and I found that very little, if any, progress was being be made. I was doing the same circuit every week and I needed to be challenged more, so changes were necessary to make it more enjoyable and challenging.   (1 mark)

I also wanted to achieve my long term goal of improving my performance as guard. I would often struggle in the latter stages of a game due to lack of stamina and frequently I could not get back to defend quickly enough. By being able to apply the principles of training to my programme, I was able to make my training more demanding by increasing the intensity and applying overload within my training.   (1 mark)

I achieved this in my training sessions by increasing the number of sets of exercises I did when working in the activity and reducing the recovery periods between each set from 1 minute to 45 seconds.   (1 mark)

Worked answers to Practice Paper A, Area 3

SKILLS AND TECHNIQUES

Question 5

(a)   Explain what you understand about information processing.   4

TOP EXAM TIP
In many of your other subjects you are asked to recall information. This means giving as much information as
you can.

HINT   Think about how you learned new skills. This will help you recall the information you took in when
learning and applying your skills during performance.

I know that information processing involves responding to a stimulus, whereby my brain sends a message to my muscles to ensure an action takes place. The brain makes sense of the action taken and the whole process starts again. This diagram shows how it works.

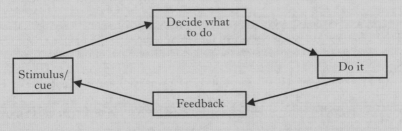

(1 mark)

I know that, when I learn skills, the above process happens extremely quickly with all four parts linked together.

Firstly, I receive information, i.e. a stimulus or cue. This could be an instruction from my coach or a movement by my team mate/opponent. Then, based on this information, I must make a decision about what action I am going to make. (1 mark)

However, in a game situation, I do not have a lot of time to think about what I am going to do as I have to act very quickly. For example, in tennis, I might think about where on the court I will place my serve, whether I will use a slice or flat or topspin shot, and where on the court I will move to, to get ready for the return. (1 mark)

Next, I get feedback about the decision I took. For example, having angled my serve cross court, did I get ready to move in to volley? Did I win the point, i.e. did I hit an ace or was it returned? Based on this outcome, the whole process starts again **instantaneously**.

I have learned that information processing is a continuous process and that the more experienced you are, the better you perform. (1 mark)

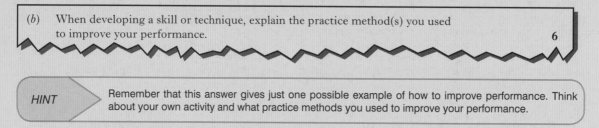

(b)   When developing a skill or technique, explain the practice method(s) you used to improve your performance.

6

> **HINT**   Remember that this answer gives just one possible example of how to improve performance. Think about your own activity and what practice methods you used to improve your performance.

To develop my tennis serve, I used a series of progressive practices.

Firstly, I used repetition drills, where I aimed at targets placed at the base of the serve box: left/centre/right. As this was in a 'closed' situation, I did not need to worry about the returned shot. This gave me a visual picture of the correct action and placement of my serve. (1 mark) I learned to reinforce my ball toss action, body positioning and follow through action. I also learned to adapt all of these according to the type of serve I selected. Changing the target that I was aiming at reinforced my ability to place and vary the tempo and depth of my serve. (1 mark)

Feedback during these repetitive drills came mainly from me – from the 'feel' of the action. If I missed the deep corner targets, then I simply aimed to get the ball anywhere in the serve box for my second serve. This took the pressure off me. I repeated this, making sure I aimed at each target 10 times. (1 mark)

I monitored my success rate and rested before I repeated the drill from the left-hand side of the court. This was necessary to ensure that I was effective from both sides. (1 mark)

I then progressed and used pressure drills. Firstly, I used the ball feed machine. With this I could adjust the speed and direction of the return, which helped to develop my follow up attacking play. As I got bored too easily by it, I only used it for a short time. (1 mark)

Finally, I used partner pressure drills, as I found them much more challenging. Playing a person, rather than a machine, made the pressure more like that experienced in a real tennis match. The game-like nature of these drills developed my ability to make better decisions. The unpredictable responses of my partner made me more alert and ready to respond with follow-up actions. My follow-up actions could be anything from moving in to volley, to staying back and engaging in a baseline rally. (1 mark)

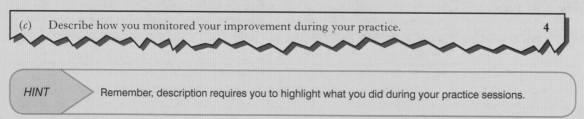

(c)   Describe how you monitored your improvement during your practice.

4

> **HINT**   Remember, description requires you to highlight what you did during your practice sessions.

I used several methods to monitor my progress during my practice sessions. Firstly, I used my initial target drill percentages to make direct comparisons. They helped me to determine which of the service techniques – topspin, slice or flat – I had more success with. I was also able to tell whether I was better on the right- or left-hand side of the court. (1 mark)

My kinaesthetic feedback allowed me to develop a better sense of 'knowing' when I had hit a good serve. I could feel and see improvements. For example, when I felt that I had placed a wide and deep topspin serve, I instantly knew to quickly follow in and finish the rally with a strong punch volley. This was happening more frequently. (1 mark)

I also filmed my performance during practice and match sessions so I could see how I looked. I then viewed this footage as many times as I needed to get feedback on errors in the subroutines of my action. When we replayed the video, I could talk over what I saw with my coach. (1 mark)

The most obvious indicators of my improvements were my match statistics. By comparing with my previous game stats, I was able to examine first serves won, double fault errors, percentage serve placements, etc.

I used all these methods to help me plan appropriate practice and ensure that I progressed. (1 mark)

(d) When developing this skill or technique, explain why feedback and motivation were important. **6**

HINT   Take each factor and offer detailed explanation to ensure you gain full marks.

Both internal and external feedback were important to ensure I placed my serves more accurately.

Internally, it was extremely important that I judged and selected the serve that would put my opponent under pressure. I could feel where my ball toss was and angle my racket at impact. (1 mark) Internal feedback helped to make me a more accomplished player as I could put all my efforts into trying for an ace serve and, if unsuccessful, vary my second serve. (1 mark)

External feedback from my coach or partner pinpointed any errors in my subroutines and helped me concentrate on the specific parts of my action. This gave me confidence to vary the pace and tempo of my delivery. (1 mark)

Motivation was essential to my improvement. Practice sessions do not always go to plan and success rate is not always easy. I had to be focussed during my target drills and motivated to reach my targets. (1 mark) During partner practice, I had to be motivated to give my best so that, if I hit a bad patch, I could refocus and concentrate by adjusting the tempo of my serve. (1 mark) Motivation was essential for getting off to a great start during match play. The more ace serves I got in, the more chance I had of winning in three sets, rather than being pushed into a punishing five-setter. (1 mark)

TOP EXAM TIP
Exams are designed to test your recall knowledge. Take a deep breath and jot down some notes from memory that will help you to tell the examiner what you know.

Question 6

Choose an activity.

(a) Explain what you understand about the stages of learning, with reference to the activity you have chosen.

6

HINT   This question is testing your knowledge of the three different stages of learning. By explaining each one in turn, and giving specific examples, you will gain full marks.

I know that there are three stages of learning. At the preparation/cognitive stage, a volleyball player will have limited understanding of how techniques are performed. Technique patterns, such as the volley and dig, can look clumsy at this stage. (1 mark) A volleyball player at this stage needs to use various types of feedback (mainly external) consistently to ensure success when he/she is learning the different techniques required to play. (1 mark)

At the practice/associative stage, I know that a volleyball player will have a good understanding of how skills/techniques are performed and show more confidence and better movement to the ball. He/She will show better co-ordination in their actions and be able to control the height of the ball when making passes. (1 mark) Also, the player can rely more on kinaesthetic/internal feedback at this stage and attempt to correct his/her technique. For example, the player can bend his/her knees and get low enough to play a dig, making sure that his/her arms are straight when lifting up. This helps him/her to attack and/or defend more quickly when in a game situation. (1 mark)

At the automatic/autonomous stage, I know that the volleyball player has a very clear understanding of how skills/techniques are performed; all of his/her passes are controlled and accurate. He/She can place his/her passes to the hitters which will enable them to spike the ball with power. (1 mark) He/She can perform a range of complex skills with good judgement. For example, when approaching the net, he/she can perfectly time his/her jump to hit his/her spike powerfully onto the opponents' side of the court. He/She communicates well and can easily play in a number of different positions. (1 mark)

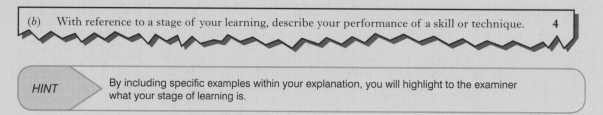

(b) With reference to a stage of your learning, describe your performance of a skill or technique. **4**

HINT By including specific examples within your explanation, you will highlight to the examiner what your stage of learning is.

As a hitter in volleyball, I feel that my performance is similar to an automatic performer.

Technically, I feel I have a range of efficient techniques. I pass the ball accurately to my team mates, which helps set up early attacks. My spike is my most powerful shot; I can easily vary the direction when I notice the opposition setting up the block. (1 mark) As I have good reaction times and good decision making skills, I know when to make my run up and communicate to my setter that I am ready to take the attack. Using good explosive power, I time my jump to get above the defence and angle my hit down and away from the block. (1 mark) Equally, if I hit against the block, I know instinctively this has happened and can drop back into position to help floor defence. This helps my team regain the attack. (1 mark) Regardless of which side of the setter I play, I can competently play my spike from the left-hand or right-hand side of the court. By using good wrist action in my follow-through, I can direct the ball cross court or down the line to wrong-foot the opposition. (1 mark)

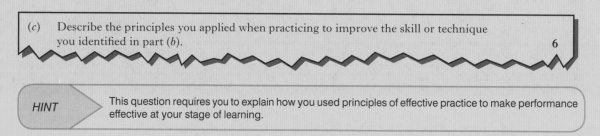

(c) Describe the principles you applied when practicing to improve the skill or technique you identified in part *(b)*. **6**

HINT This question requires you to explain how you used principles of effective practice to make performance effective at your stage of learning.

When developing my spike, I knew to consider a range of principles that were important to ensure success. One of the things I considered was the type of practice that would be most effective for my stage of learning. As I was at the automatic stage, I knew to include pressure and game-like practices to ensure that I would cope better once in my game role. (1 mark)

I had to decide on the number of drills that I would include; the type of feedback I would get once my targets had been reached; rest periods; and variation of my drills to keep me motivated. (1 mark)

Once I had selected the best type of practice for me, and by that I mean the most enjoyable and motivating, I set realistic targets that I wanted to achieve. For example, in the set, block and hit pressure drill, the first 10 sets I returned could be placed fairly accurately to the sidelines. I had to aim the next 10 cross court to improve my angle and direction and to increase the pressure. (1 mark)

I knew to take rest periods which helped me regain focus and assess my success rate. My coach and an observation record sheet gave me the feedback necessary to refine my technique. (1 mark)

To make me more successful, I repeated this pressure drill but did it from the harder left-hand angle. I tried to hit the ball with my left hand so that I would become as successful with my left hand as with my right. (1 mark)

By varying the pressure drills, I was motivated to do well. My ability to read the game and anticipate how the block would be set up against me improved, and I felt that I was more confident in my ability to spike at various angles. I always monitored any improvements by looking at my recent match statistics. (1 mark)

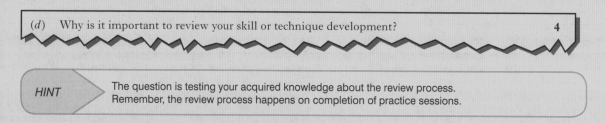

(d) Why is it important to review your skill or technique development? **4**

HINT The question is testing your acquired knowledge about the review process. Remember, the review process happens on completion of practice sessions.

Not only did the review process ensure I got the best out of each practice session during my training period, it was also really motivating, and kept me on track and determined to succeed. Also, when my practice period was completely finished, I knew that it was very important to evaluate whether I was now better than before.

(1 mark).

At the start of my training, I set targets to improve both my right-hand and left-hand side spike. Reviewing my results gave me concrete feedback, as I compared my first statistics to my last. It was also important for me to look at both my practice and game statistics because this gave me the full picture of my accuracy and points won.

(1 mark)

Talking to my coach was also important as it supported my own feelings and helped me evaluate whether my drills were pitched at the right level for me. In other words, whether they were specific. I asked myself the following types of questions: Have I selected the right type of drills? Have I made the right progressions? Am I consistent?

(1 mark)

At the end, I was able to judge whether to continue to work on my spike technique or address other weaknesses that I had. It also gave me the confidence to offer advice to others about what worked for me, which may have given them ideas to include in their training.

(1 mark)

TOP EXAM TIP

If you made 'memory jogger' notes at the start, check that you have included **all** the points you wanted to include.

Worked answers to Practice Paper A, Area 4

STRUCTURES, STRATEGIES AND COMPOSITION

TOP EXAM TIP

Remember – in this area of analysis 'you' can refer to 'you' as an individual or 'you' as a team. Try to make which it is clear in your answer.

Question 7

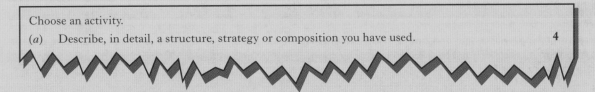

Choose an activity.

(a)   Describe, in detail, a structure, strategy or composition you have used.   **4**

The activity that I have chosen is basketball. The strategy that we have used is half court man-to-man defence. In this strategy each member of my team is responsible for marking an opponent as soon as they come into our half of the court. The main job for each person is to prevent their player from receiving the ball and from scoring a basket.

(1 mark)

There are three key roles to adopt in this strategy. These are 'ball', 'help' and 'deny'. In defending, it is important to keep between your player and the basket at all times. If I am playing 'ball' defence, I am marking the player with the ball and I want to prevent them from passing to a team mate or dribbling past me or shooting.

(1 mark)

If I am playing 'deny', I am usually one pass away from the person who has the ball. My job is to mark my player tightly and prevent them from receiving a pass from the person who has the ball.

(1 mark)

Finally, if I am playing 'help' defence, it means that my job is to help a team mate who has lost the player they were marking and who is now a threat to my team. I can, if possible, move to put pressure on this player and so prevent a clear path to the basket.

(1 mark)

(b)   What factors did you take into consideration before selecting this structure, strategy
       or composition? Give examples to support your answer.   **6**

First of all we considered the strengths and weaknesses of our own team. In order to play this strategy, it is important, when players match up against an opponent, that they are able to defend as tightly as possible without being too aggressive and picking up fouls. A team does not want to keep picking up fouls or it will have players fouled out. So we made sure we put on players who could carry out this role without fouling.   (1 mark)

We also considered the fitness level of our team. Half court man-to-man defence can be very demanding so we had to make sure that our fitness level was high. We had to consider how long each defender could last before they needed to be subbed, or how long we could apply the strategy before it needed to be changed.   (1 mark)

We also considered the strengths and weaknesses of the opposition. It was important to match up against our opponents. For example, we would make sure that our tallest players would mark their tallest so that there was no mismatch when rebounding the ball. We would also make sure that we put our best defender on their strongest player to prevent them from receiving the ball or from driving to the basket.   (1 mark)

We also considered the previous time that we had played against our opponents and had used half court man-to-man defence. We knew each player's skills and what they were good or poor at. For example, they had a ball carrier who set up the play and who was not strong on his left hand, so we made sure whoever was marking him tried to force him to dribble using that hand.   (1 mark)

The previous time we played them also gave us information on what offence they might play against our half court man-to-man defence. We were able to reflect on whether our defence strategy had been successful or not. We could then go back and work in practice on weaknesses that we had identified.   (1 mark)

Finally, we would consider the time and score in the game. If we were losing and needed to put pressure on the opposition, and then we would probably decide to use this strategy.   (1 mark)

> **HINT**   In a non-team activity your considerations will be different. Give as much detail as you can to access full marks.

(c)   Briefly describe a situation where you had to **adapt** or **change** your structure, strategy or
       composition. Explain why these changes or adaptations made your performance more effective.   **6**

> **TOP EXAM TIP**
> 'Explain' questions require more development than 'describe' questions.

When we were playing against our opposition, they had two very good forwards who continually beat our defenders who were marking them. They were able to drive to the basket. This led to them scoring baskets and us losing the game.   (1 mark)

This also put pressure on the rest of the defenders as they had to try to help out where possible or we had to foul them to stop them dribbling. This led to our players and team being in foul trouble.   (1 mark)

As a team, we changed our strategy and switched to 2-1-2 zone defence. This meant that each player had to mark a particular space rather than a player. The zone is a tight structure and prevented the forwards from making easy drives to the basket as there was very little space available.   (1 mark)

If a forward did manage to enter the zone, there was always another player waiting to stop them. As each defender's space to mark in the zone overlapped, the forwards were always faced with defenders. This forced the forward to try to pass the ball or make a difficult shot under pressure.   (1 mark)

The zone defence also cut down the number of fouls that each player and the team picked up. Players were now less likely to foul, compared to when they were marking individual players. Our defenders knew they always had help in the zone if they could not prevent a player from entering their space.   (1 mark)

Finally, as a team, we lost fewer easy baskets and made it more difficult for the opposition to score by using a zone defence. As the opposition were not able to drive to the basket very often, they had to resort to passing the ball round the key and trying to get a basket by shooting from outside our zone which was difficult for them.   (1 mark)

> **HINT**   In this question you are being asked to answer two parts with different command words: 'describe' and 'explain'. Make sure that you address both parts to access full marks.

(*d*)   Describe how you evaluated your changes or adaptations to see if they had been successful.   **4**

We first of all took game data on our new strategy by filling in a game analysis sheet. This showed every time a basket had been scored against us and how it had happened. This sheet had all the possible situations in a game, for example outside shot, drive to basket, fast break rebound, etc.   (1 mark)

We also filmed the game on video and used this along with the game analysis sheet. This made the results more accurate as, in a game, the action is fast and you can often miss baskets.   (1 mark)

The data we gained was then compared to data that had been taken previously, when using half court man-to-man defence. The methods used were the same except for the different criteria on the game analysis sheet. This gave us information as to the effectiveness of our new strategy, compared to the previous one.   (1 mark)

Finally, from the data collected we could also reflect on our new strategy and see which parts were effective. Also, we could see where and if the strategy broke down. This allowed us to identify weaknesses that we could then work on in training.   (1 mark)

> **HINT**   These are only some examples of evaluation methods. You may be able to think of other examples that you have used.

Question 8

(*a*)   Describe a structure, strategy or composition you have used in an **individual** activity of your choice.   **4**

The strategy that I have chosen is the serve volley in tennis. The strategy involves executing a fast and powerful service into my opponent's service box on my first serve. This will immediately put pressure on my opponent.   (1 mark)

I need to be able to predict where my serve will land in my opponent's service box. Then, it is important for me to get quickly into a position near the net where I am able to meet the return of my opponent and finish the point off with a volley.   (1 mark)

I immediately follow my serve into the net and try to finish the point by volleying my opponent's return of serve into the opposite side of the court, either using a forehand or backhand punch volley, or by taking the pace off the return using a stop volley, landing the ball just over the net.   (1 mark)

When serving, I can change the direction of the serve by altering the pace on the ball using a top spin or slice serve. I can also change the placement of the serve by changing the angle of my body when serving.   (1 mark)

> **HINT**   Remember – this question is asking about an individual activity. Be careful not to use a team activity. Use activities like tennis, swimming, gymnastics or dance, otherwise you will gain no marks.

(*b*)   Describe how you collected data on your performance when applying this structure, strategy or composition. Why were the methods you used appropriate?   **4**

When using this strategy in tennis, I used a video in conjunction with a match analysis sheet on the effectiveness of my serve volley strategy when playing in actual games. I collected data, marking down each time I used my serve volley strategy and finding out how many points I won outright using the strategy.   (1 mark)

I also collected data on the types of serve and volley that I used in games. I got a classmate to fill in an observation schedule on the type of serve I used and whether my opponent had to use a forehand or backhand return. For the volley, they had to collect data on the type of volley used and the outcome of that shot.   (1 mark)

The video and match analysis sheet were appropriate because I could gain clear evidence on the success rate of my serve volley technique. I could also watch my performance repeatedly and find out information on my serve and volley strengths and weaknesses.   (1 mark)

The observation schedule was appropriate as it allowed me to gain valuable information on which type of serve and volley were the most and least successful. It was also always taken from games so that I was serving and volleying under actual game pressure.   (1 mark)

> *HINT*   No marks are given for simply naming the methods you used to gather information.

(c)   Briefly describe the weaknesses you found in the structure, strategy or composition from the data collected. Discuss the course of action you took to address these weaknesses.   6

TOP EXAM TIP

Reading each question carefully is crucial. There are two parts to this question so remember to answer both. Marks are lost through not reading the question.

From the data I discovered that my backhand volley was weak. This was because my body angle was wrong and my racket position was poor. I often played the ball level with my body instead of out in front. This caused me to be less accurate and hit many volleys out of court.   (1 mark)

I also had a poor second serve. Often it was too short in length. This allowed my opponent to either hit a powerful return past me as I approached the net, or return the ball low to my feet, forcing me to play the ball into the net.   (1 mark)

In order to improve my backhand volley, I designed a series of training drills. I had a feeder throw balls to my backhand side. I would concentrate on angling my body and turning my shoulder to meet the ball in front of me. By repeating this movement I got used to an improved technique. Gradually the speed and the distance of the throw increased so I was put under pressure.   (1 mark)

I then carried out a more pressurised drill. I used a feeder to hit the ball to me. I had to start from the service 'T' and move into position to play a backhand volley. I had to aim for targets set up on the baseline. This was designed to improve my accuracy as well as my movement pattern for playing the volley.   (1 mark)

To improve my second serve, I aimed for targets which were placed near the end of my opponent's service box. This would get me to serve deeper making it a little more difficult for my opponent to return the ball. It also gave me a little more time to get into position to play my next shot.   (1 mark)

I also learned to vary my second service. I learned how to put top spin on the ball when serving. This is where the service gathers pace after it hits the court. I practised by repeating the action frequently. This variation on serve can catch an opponent by surprise and put them under pressure, often forcing them into errors.   (1 mark)

(d)   Structures, strategies and compositions are based on certain key principles/ fundamentals. Select **two** that you have used and explain their importance when applying your structure, strategy or composition.   6

The first principle I used was speed/tempo in play. My target was to serve fast and then go into the net to volley a winner from my opponent's return. However, there were times when I needed to vary the speed depending on particular circumstances. If my opponent was very good at returning my first serve, and often passed me at the net, I decided to take some pace off my serve to give me more time to get into the net or alternatively forced my opponent out wide on service.   (1 mark)

I sometimes also decided to stay back on service rather than go into the net. I played from the baseline and played some shots from the back of the court. I could vary the pace and direction of these shots, and not allow my opponent to get into a rhythm. By varying the pace, I could either slow the game down or speed it up, and try to force my opponent into making errors.   (1 mark)

I also discovered my opponent was poor on returning using his backhand. I decided to target that side as often as possible. I wanted to make sure my first serve was in so I decided to use a slower first serve and use more slice on the serve. This meant that my opponent had to use his backhand and he often lost points by failing to return the serve.   (1 mark)

The second principle/fundamental I used was creativity. I wanted to catch my opponent unawares by being creative. I tried to serve and follow into the net and volley the return as usual but, instead of punching the volley deep, I played a stop volley by just dropping the ball over the net, making it very difficult for my opponent to reach.   (1 mark)

I also tried to be creative by changing my tactics. I sometimes stayed back after serving and tried to play a drop shot just over the net, forcing my opponent to come into the net to return the shot. I then played a lob from his return over his head and hopefully make an outright winner or force him into a mistake.   (1 mark)

Finally, after I served and went into the net to volley the return, I would try to be creative by making my opponent think I was going to play the ball to a particular side of the court and at the last moment change my body angle and racket position and return the ball to the opposite side, wrong footing my opponent.   (1 mark)

| HINT | This question is quite demanding as it is asking you to think about two principles/fundamentals and their influence on a structure, strategy or composition you have used. You must ensure your answer does this to be able to gain good marks. |

PERFORMANCE APPRECIATION

Question 1

Choose an activity.

(a) Why is goal setting important for your performance improvement? **4**

TOP EXAM TIP

Read the whole question before starting your answer. It is important you have an understanding about *all* parts of the question to ensure you access full marks.

HINT

The question is asking for your acquired knowledge about the purpose of goal setting. By establishing the link between short and long term goals, and justifying your reasons, you will be using your critical thinking skills.

Goal setting is very important when working to improve performance. To be successful I know that I need to set short term goals before aiming for longer term ones. For example, a short term goal might be to get ready for a weekend game, whereas a long term goal might be to prepare for an inter-school tournament. (1 mark) Goal setting can be linked to stages of learning. For example, to improve it is important to set goals that are specific to my weaknesses so that I select practices or fitness training at the right level for my stage of learning. (1 mark) Goal setting keeps me motivated, determined and committed to achieving success. I am able to monitor this success by comparing new performances to earlier ones. (1 mark) Setting goals also gives me confidence and personal satisfaction and helps me set future targets, not just in sport but in everyday life. (1 mark)

(b) Outline the methods you used to collect data on your performance in an activity. Explain what your analysis of the data showed. **6**

HINT

The question is in two parts. The first part asks for a brief outline of the methods you used – make sure you link this to the specific focus of performance. The second part requires you to interpret what the data revealed.

TOP EXAM TIP

Specific examples strengthen your answer. There are many types of data collection – the methods of data collection used in this answer are only two examples.

The data collection methods I used included video and match analysis sheets – both were valid methods.

I wanted to find out how effective I was in my role as a wing defence in netball.

The video was taken for the whole game and followed my contributions as a wing defence. I watched this several times which let me check my match analysis sheets to see if they backed up what I was viewing in the video. (1 mark)

The match analysis was divided into five-minute slots for each of the four quarters. I asked my marker to indicate the number of passes I made, the number of passes I tipped or intercepted, and the number of times I forced my partner to commit a foul or time violation. (1 mark)

When I analysed both the video and match analysis sheets, I was able to look at my strengths and weaknesses in my role as wing defence. The analysis of my data showed that I performed most of my defensive duties well. My percentage of interceptions, blocks and forced time violations were high, especially at the centre pass. (1 mark)

I was not so consistent when performing my attacking duties. When our own goal attack and wing attack were being tightly marked, I should have been ready to get out and take the pass that was intended for them. I was slow to react to my centre, who required assistance, and caused her to time violate. (1 mark) I also mistimed my long feed into the circle and did not take enough notice of our opponents' goal defence; this meant I was throwing away potential shooting opportunities. I could see this first hand from the video action. (1 mark) On too many occasions I was slow to react to loose balls and failed to get further up court to support back passes from my goal attack and wing attack. (1 mark)

(c)   In relation to your data analysis, describe, in detail, a training programme you used to
     develop your performance.   6

TOP EXAM TIP

Remember, in Performance Appreciation you can focus on any area of your performance for further development; for example, skill improvement, physical skill, mental fitness development or strategic development. Using diagrams can support your answer.

HINT   Make logical connections to your data analysis when describing the training programme used. Remember, there are lots of different types of training that could be used. You will get top marks for selecting the most relevant for your identified need.

As I could see from my data, I needed to improve my assist play and support my goal attack and wing attack. I also needed to improve my long range passes into the circle. As these weaknesses were game related, I used a series of repetition and pressure drills. This was specific as it allowed me to work on quicker off the mark movement up the court and improve my ability to time and throw longer shoulder passes. (1 mark)

I set up the repetition drill (a) of running from my centre third line to receive a pass from my centre. I then passed a long ball into the shooting circle to my goal shooter or goal attack. I did this ten times without defenders and then repeated with defenders marking. (1 mark) To ensure pass accuracy, I varied the distance between myself and the shooters. I also made sure that the shooters made their run into the circle to improve my timing and anticipation of their speed into space (see diagram). Again, I did this ten times with and without defenders. (1 mark) I set realistic targets and made sure I monitored weaknesses as well as improvements. I got feedback from my centre in particular and I checked my match analysis sheets to be sure I was improving.

(1 mark)

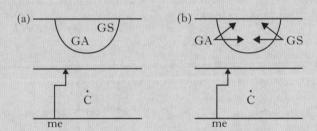

I also included pressure drills to make me react quicker. In a 3v3 situation, we had to make ten passes in a row. I then had to get free and take the last pass; I also had to time my long shoulder pass to one of three designated areas. (1 mark)

Finally, at centre pass repetition drills I had both the WA and opposing C double mark me; this speeded up my reaction time and made me more determined to succeed. My job was to get free to receive and release the best option pass. During my skill training, I had to make sure my drills were realistic and that I took proper rest periods. (1 mark)

(d)   Explain how your performance was affected on completion of your training.   4

TOP EXAM TIP

Think back to how you felt once your training was over. Starting your answer with an immediate statement will help you to justify your opinion.

HINT   Make logical connections to the training used and reflect on previous data analysis and statistics.

I know that the training had a positive impact on my performance. I definitely felt sharper, more confident and a better support player. (1 mark) Comparing the video and match analysis sheets, I could see my success rate at delivering long ball feeds into the shooting circle was much higher. I believe that this was because my practice drills had focused on releasing the ball earlier and faster. (1 mark) At centre passes it was more noticeable that, even when not used in the first ball attack, I was there, ready and waiting to support play. I was always behind my goal attack and wing attack and shouted to them 'here if you need me'. (1 mark) My court movement on and off the ball is much faster, I now rarely get substituted and get high praise from my team mates. I always feature in the starting seven and enjoy my games much more. (1 mark)

TOP EXAM TIP

Adopt a positive attitude toward being tested. This is your chance to show how much you've learned.

Question 2

Choose an activity.

(a) Explain why it can be easier to perform during training/practice sessions than in competitive situations.

4

HINT The question tests your acquired knowledge about the different factors that can affect performance. The content of your answer may include detail in relation to both internal and external pressures.

During my badminton practice there is less pressure on me to do well. My opponents may not necessarily be as good as me or be trying their hardest to beat me. It is more relaxing and I usually feel in control and confident. I often feel as though I could never make a mistake. (1 mark) Although I try to perform my skills effectively, the practice regime allows me to apply, or at least try, a fuller repertoire of shots; therefore I do not have to worry about varying shots as much. (1 mark)

In competition, however, I am under greater pressure. My opponents are as determined as me to win. As well as dealing with internal factors such as handling my emotions, maintaining my confidence, etc., I also have to cope with many external factors affecting performance. For example, my parents often come to watch me play; although I find this encouraging, it sometimes makes me nervous. (1 mark) I worry about the opponents I face and this sometimes intimidates me. I tighten up, the consistency of my shots drops and my decision making is not as sharp. Before I know it, I lose three to four points in quick succession. (1 mark)

(b) Describe, in detail, how you gathered information on your performance either during training sessions or in the competitive performance situation. Why is this important?

6

HINT It does not matter whether you select training or competition. You will show related knowledge by describing the most appropriate, valid and reliable methods. For full marks you must justify why it is important to go through this process.

The data methods I used were a video, match analysis sheets and specific questionnaire sheet.

I wanted to find out how effectively I performed in my singles. Specifically, I wanted to know if I performed my defending and attacking play consistently throughout the game. I decided to use the video as this was the best tool of analysis to avoid human error. (1 mark) The game is fast paced and I did not want to miss anything. The video allowed me to look at my game several times, which let me check my match analysis and questionnaire sheets to see if they corresponded with my performance in the video. (1 mark)

The match analysis sheet was divided into change of serve slots for the duration of the game. I asked my marker to indicate my court coverage, serve placement and point won or lost when playing a smash, drop or net shot. This was important as it let me analyse which shots were effective. (1 mark)

My questionnaire was designed specifically to evaluate my mental fitness. The specificity of the questions related to my success rate at controlling my temper, especially after making unforced errors or when the score was tight. (1 mark)

Gathering this data and noting my match results were important for reviewing my abilities and working towards making my performance better. (1 mark) They were an excellent source of motivation as I could look back on how I defeated some of my opponents. This meant I had a permanent record, as I worked up the rankings. (1 mark)

(c) With reference to a specific competitive performance, describe what you did to try to ensure you performed to the best of your ability.

6

> **HINT** This question can be answered either in terms of planning your training or practice to make sure you were ready to give your best, or within the context of managing a competitive situation. You can show what you did tactically, mentally or physically to make sure you performed well.

Playing in the last 16 of the nationals was important as I desperately wanted to win. I had worked hard on my fitness and preparation for this competition. This preparation was essential to ensure I was at my peak performance. (1 mark) From my knowledge of his previous performance, I knew my opponent's strengths and prepared a solid game plan to get off to a quick attack and secure a 3/4 point lead. I have a wide range of technical skills, and so, to get this early lead, I took my time and varied my serve placement which affected my opponent's balance. (1 mark) I played out the rallies with good control. I attacked aggressively when the options were presented, smashing deep, and shut out the intimidation created by my opponent. (1 mark) My earlier mental training helped me during the tighter rallies; taking deep breaths and tapping my racket against my thigh pumped me up and helped me regain focus. (1 mark) Creating good chances, however, was not always down to me. I had to react quickly to my opponent's strategy and outwit him by anticipating shots and using good court coverage to get back and cover the T. (1 mark) My hard work in fitness training paid off. I was fast, agile and had a good range of flexibility to reach drop shots, and high levels of cardio-respiratory endurance to defend consistently. (1 mark)

(d) For future performance development, outline (a) performance goal(s) you would set. Briefly describe how you would achieve this (these).

4

> **HINT** Starting your answer with the question will help you to provide detail and give structure to your answer.

My main goal is to continue with maintaining my general fitness levels and work on refining my shots so that I am ready for the last stages of the finals. (1 mark) My opponents get harder in the latter stages of the tournament so it is crucial that I remain sharp and keep consistent in the delivery of my shots. (1 mark)

To do this, I will continue with court drills which specifically work on good balance and court movement, as well as developing my speed endurance. (1 mark) During repetition drills and pressure drills I will try for even greater accuracy and disguise on my drop and net shots, using hoops. I will aim to hit these targets before finishing with a match-type game. (1 mark)

> **TOP EXAM TIP**
> Take time to re-read your answer. This will help you add in any information you may have missed.

Worked answers to Practice Paper B, Area 2

PREPARATION OF THE BODY

Question 3

(a) Select an aspect of fitness important to your activity and describe how you gathered information on this aspect of fitness both **within** and **outwith** your activity.

6

> **TOP EXAM TIP**
> Descriptions need detail – not just the basics. Adding examples is a great idea.

> **HINT** Select methods you have used during your practical sessions. Remember, this question is asking for two different methods of gathering information. Look carefully at the words in bold to make sure you answer this question fully.

The activity I have chosen is football and the aspect of fitness selected is cardio-respiratory endurance. This is important as I play midfield and want to be able to keep going for the entire 90 minutes.

Outwith the activity, to gather information I used the bleep test which is a nationally recognised test. Two sets of cones were placed 20 metres apart. I had to run continuously between the two sets of cones in time to recorded bleeps on a CD. (1 mark) I started off standing behind one of the lines and had to run to the other cones before the next bleep sounded. The speed at first was quite slow. (1 mark) The time between the bleeps gradually decreased so I had to run quicker as the test progressed. If I did not make it to the cones on two consecutive occasions before the next bleep then I had to finish. My results were recorded and measured against national norms.   (1 mark)

Within the activity, I gathered information by using a timed match analysis sheet in conjunction with a video. I played a full game and got a friend of mine to video my performance during the game. This meant I could replay this later and fill in my match analysis sheet.   (1 mark)

The sheet consisted, down one side, of each half broken into 15-minute slots, being 0–15, 15–30, 30–45, 45–60, 60–75 and 75–90 minutes. At the top of the sheet were words describing walking or running speed and relating to CRE (see table below).   (1 mark)

Time in minutes	Walking	Jogging	Half pace running	Sprinting
0–15				
15–30				
30–45				
45–60				
60–75				
75–90				

After the match I played back the video and recorded each time I did one of the actions above. I did this by using a tick in the appropriate column. I had a time clock on my video which made sure I could record each action within the correct time section.   (1 mark)

(b)   Explain why it is important to collect information on your fitness before planning a
        training programme.   4

It is important to gather information about my fitness as it can provide accurate and objective fitness information about me in relation to the demands of my role in the game or activity. For example, in football I could gather information on my CRE as my role is midfield player.   (1 mark)

I can then get information on my strengths and weaknesses. This information provides me with a benchmark to work from and can be used to plan my training programme.   (1 mark)

Using this information also means that I am able to set realistic and achievable short and long term targets for fitness improvements over a planned period of time in my training programme.   (1 mark)

Finally, I can use this information to compare results after my training programme to those results I obtained at the start of my programme. This will give me information on whether my level of fitness has improved and whether my training programme has been effective.   (1 mark)

(c)   Discuss how you applied the principles of training when planning a programme to improve
        the aspect of fitness selected in part (a).   6

The first principle that I applied when planning my training programme was specificity. I made sure that, having collected information on my level of fitness, my programme was based on my strengths and weaknesses in the particular aspect of fitness to be improved, as well as on the demands of the activity.   (1 mark)

I then looked at how often I would train (frequency) and decided that I would carry out my training over an eight-week period to give myself enough time to make improvements. I also decided to train during my PE periods and to go to the gym once per week to do some circuits. (1 mark)

I trained within the activity, doing a mixture of running and game-related drills to not only improve my fitness, but also my skills in the game. I trained for one hour (duration) for each of the two periods of PE and also I did gym work for at least 25 minutes to try to keep within my training zone. (1 mark)

In my training, I did continuous running for 20 minutes in the first few weeks but, as my level of CRE improved, I decided to increase this by five minutes. In my circuit in the gym, I did two sets of exercises specifically to improve CRE. After week 4, I increased the sets to three and later in my programme also reduced the recovery between each set to 35 seconds instead of 45. This ensured I was applying the principle of overload to my training programme. (1 mark)

I also made sure that, when I was training, I was keeping within my training zone. This ensured that my training was effective. It was important that my heart rate was always between 146–168 beats per minute. (1 mark)

This ensured progression in my programme and put my body under more stress, therefore improving all aspects of my work. By using these principles, my programme was progressive. (1 mark)

(d)   Discuss the effects that your training had on your performance.   **4**

First of all I was able to sustain a higher-level and more consistent performance for longer before fatigue set in. I was able to keep running for longer and I was in better condition towards the end of the game because of my improved level of CRE. (1 mark)

I was still managing to support the attack in the later stages of the game, making myself available for passes from teammates or getting into forward positions more often to try to score a goal. (1 mark)

When defending, I was able to stay with the player that I was marking; also, when required, I was able to get back quickly to help out the defence if they were under pressure. I was also on hand to receive a pass out of defence to try to start a new attack. (1 mark)

Finally, because I felt fitter, I was more motivated and confident in my performance. This led to a better overall performance throughout the final stages of the game. I felt that my level of skill was more consistent than it had been before I carried out my training programme. (1 mark)

Question 4

Choose an activity.
(a)   Physical, skill-related and mental fitness are important for effective performance within your activity. Select **one** aspect of **each type** of fitness and explain its importance for effective performance.   **6**

The activity I have chosen is badminton and the aspect of physical fitness selected is speed endurance. Having good speed endurance means that I can get to the shuttle quickly. I am also able to return to base position ready for the next shot from my opponent, throughout long rallies and throughout the match. (1 mark)

Without a high level of speed endurance, I will get out of breath quickly and tire easily during long rallies. This will lead to mistakes being made and also allow my opponent the upper hand during rallies, which will result in me losing the point.   (1 mark)

The aspect of skill-related fitness I have chosen is agility. Agility is a combination of speed and flexibility and enables me to change direction and the speed at which I am travelling quickly and efficiently. This allows me to move around the court quickly to reach and retrieve the shuttle.   (1 mark)

Agility also allows me to reach all corners of the court and to cover the whole court effectively. I can then recover quickly to my central base to be ready for the next shot that my opponent is going to play.   (1 mark)

The aspect of mental fitness I have chosen is determination. This aspect is important as allows me to mentally keep going throughout the match no matter what is happening. If I have good determination I will not go down without a fight and can keep the pace and the accuracy of my shots going until the very last point in the game.
                                                                                                                                                   (1 mark)

Also having good determination means that I have the 'will to win' and remain focused on the game. I am not put off by distractions and will try hard to maintain my performance and beat my opponent. I will not give up easily and will put maximum effort into every point.   (1 mark)

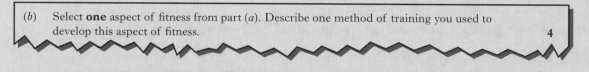

(b)   Select **one** aspect of fitness from part (a). Describe one method of training you used to develop this aspect of fitness.   4

> **HINT**   The answer provides an example of one method of training. There are many methods you could use. Think of the different methods you may have used to improve an aspect of fitness.

I used interval training to improve my speed and endurance.

Interval training can be best described as bouts of exercise interspersed with short rest intervals. Very short, all-out bouts of work coupled with longer rest periods are used for speed and speed endurance development.
                                                                                                                                                   (1 mark)

I decided to train twice per week and work for between 20–30 minutes per session on improving my speed endurance. I trained during my PE lessons at school and used the badminton court.   (1 mark)

I carried out the following during my training programme:
1.   Held a racket, stood at one far corner of the court (where baseline and doubles sideline meet).
2.   Side stepped along the baseline to the other far corner.
3.   Ran three quarter pace diagonally across the court to the corner of the net. Made an imaginary forehand drop shot with the racket.
4.   Side stepped along the length of the net to the final corner.
5.   Turned and ran at three quarter pace diagonally across the court back to the start. Made an imaginary overhead clear shot.   (1 mark)

I continued this sequence for 60 seconds then rested for one to two minutes. I performed a total of five runs to complete one set. I rested for three minutes and repeated for two to three sets.   (1 mark)

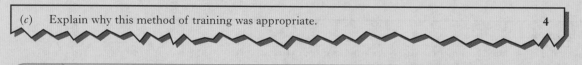

(c)   Explain why this method of training was appropriate.   4

> **HINT**   Don't be afraid to refer back to the method used and give an example of what you did to highlight why the method was appropriate.

This method of training was appropriate because it helped to develop both aerobic and anaerobic fitness. This allowed me to sprint faster during rallies so that I could reach the shuttle and recover more quickly between points.
                                                                                                                                                   (1 mark)

Interval training also allowed me to vary the time or distance of each period of exercise or the amount of effort I put into each exercise. It also allowed me to vary the recovery time or number of sets in each session.

(1 mark)

Because each session could be varied, it made training more enjoyable and, also, I could do this training during my lessons on the actual badminton court which made it easy to organise.

(1 mark)

Finally, interval training allowed me to train and play for longer periods of time. The high intensity work meant that my fitness level progressed quickly, allowing me to keep playing at a high tempo for longer.

(1 mark)

(d) Discuss the importance of setting goals to improve your level of fitness. Give examples of goals you have set.

6

> HINT — Remember, discussion requires you to offer an opinion and justify why it is important to set goals. You need to describe what your goals help you to achieve, not just state them.

It is important that I set myself goals so that I have a target to work towards when I am carrying out my training programme. These goals must be realistic and achievable, otherwise they will be impossible to reach.

(1 mark)

Setting goals is a good way to motivate yourself to work hard when you are training. This will help you get through those times when you find training hard. You feel a sense of achievement when you manage to see an improvement in your fitness, which hopefully will show in your performance when playing.

(1 mark)

It is important to set short and long term goals, so that you have something that you can measure in both the short and long term. Short term goals enable me to monitor my training and determine whether my programme is working and whether I can then go on to achieve my long term goal.

(1 mark)

My short term goal was to try to improve my position in the badminton ladder. At the beginning of the course I was in tenth place out of fourteen in the class. I often lost close games because I became tired in the later stages of rallies. I managed to achieve this goal and ended up two places higher in the ladder.

(1 mark)

Finally, setting goals allowed me to record progress on my fitness and gave me the incentive to work hard, not only to improve my level of fitness but also my overall performance. Matches are often won and lost due to poor fitness, especially in close games in the final stages, so, if I could achieve my goals, I would win more games.

(1 mark)

My long term goal was to pass my performance unit in badminton and also to beat two friends in the class who I had previously lost to, 2 games to 1. The previous scores were very close with me losing 11–8 in the final game to both of them. I was determined to achieve my goal. I managed to beat one of them but just narrowly lost to the other – but I passed my unit.

(1 mark)

Worked answers to Practice Paper B, Area 3

SKILLS AND TECHNIQUES

Question 5

Choose an activity.
(a) Describe **two** methods you used to gather information on your performance of skills or techniques.

4

> HINT — Select methods you have used during your practical sessions. This will help you to describe the detail and highlight reliability and validity issues.

When practising my gymnastics routine, I used a technique observation sheet and a video. Both these methods were reliable as the footage could be replayed, allowing me more time to compare against the criteria on my observation sheets. (1 mark)

The observation sheet contained a list of all my technical skills, both simple and complex. Against these techniques there was a column and, using a tick or cross, two observers completed observation sheets to show which ones I performed well at and which ones I needed to improve. (1 mark)

At the bottom of this sheet was a comment box for my trained observers to highlight how effectively I used variations of rhythm, direction and weight to make my sequence more interesting. This was marked on a scale 1–4 which I could see at a glance. (1 mark)

I also performed my sequence several times and had it video recorded. This helped me to compare my performance against model performers'. I then got valuable feedback on how effectively I had performed during my sequence. The video is an excellent source as it shows the live performance and so nothing can be missed out. (1 mark)

(b)   From your analysis of this information, describe your skill development needs.   **4**

> HINT   Outline specific parts of your performance requiring improvement.

After analysing and discussing with my observers, I felt I demonstrated good control and fluency; my routine was imaginative with good timing. I showed effectiveness in a range of my techniques. However, when I used my one-handed cartwheel I felt I lost shape and form. (1 mark)

In my routine, I used the cartwheel to vary my rhythm and change direction in my sequence. As I moved out of my cartwheel I added on a dive forward roll to change pathways. It looked unsteady, especially as I moved into the transition phase of the cartwheel technique. (1 mark)

Having compared my performance to a model performer's, I was able to see that I lost the shape and form in my cartwheel because I did not accelerate quickly enough into my approach run, or apply sufficient force off the ground to get my legs and hips above my base. (1 mark) This affected my balance and I then had problems moving into my dive forward roll. Sometimes I would be too fast and over rotated, sometimes I did not have sufficient speed so my forward roll looked uncontrolled. (1 mark) Therefore improvements in my cartwheel were definitely needed.

(c)   Discuss the practice programme you used to improve your skill development.   **6**

I used a gradual build up practice programme to help me make my sequence look more technically correct. I used repetition practice at first. This let me practice my cartwheel in isolation. I started with a two-handed cartwheel so that I could build up my confidence and get my balance correct. (1 mark) Once competent, I progressed to lifting one hand. I did several repeats until I could judge the speed of acceleration into the cartwheel. This gave me more time to think about my shape when in the air and reinforce the 'feel' of what I was doing. (1 mark) I had to consider rest periods as it was very tiring performing this complex technique. I also got feedback during the rest periods which kept me motivated to do better. (1 mark)

I then practised the dive forward roll but only very briefly as this was a simple technique and I could quickly manage this in isolation. The hard part was linking both techniques together to make it look like one. I then combined my one-handed cartwheel with my dive forward roll. I used mental rehearsal and, in my head, quickly ran through the running at full speed and placing my hand on the target spot to get height and shape. (1 mark)

This was a good way of practising, as I could feel improvements and rely on my internal feedback to ensure good timing, shape and form. I was then ready to put this combined sequence back into my whole floorwork routine so that I would be working in competition mode. (1 mark)

At the end of this practice session. I reviewed my sequence on video to note improvements and see if there were still some things I could do to make my routine more interesting. This also increased my self belief that I could do well in competition. (1 mark)

(d) Discuss the effect of your practice methods on your whole performance. Why may there still be (a) weakness(es) in your performance?

6

HINT Remember – discussion requires you to offer opinion and justify how your whole performance benefited as a result of your practice programme. For full marks you also need to think critically about any weaknesses that may still exist.

I believe my practice method was appropriate as the repetitive nature allowed me to progress at my own pace. It also enabled me to build up my confidence and mental awareness as I more readily used visualisation, going over my sequence in my head before I started. (1 mark) When performing in competition, I need to get as many points for my floorwork routine as I can because my vault is less reliable. As a result of my practice, I perform my sequence with more control, flair, rhythm and fluency. (1 mark) The shape of my legs when in the flight phase is much more streamlined and my dive forward roll is much higher and faster, which lets me link into my next skill sequence more fluently. (1 mark) During my practice, I was able to practise with different types and tempos of music. This helped me create a more complex choreographic design and so I gained more artistic points.

(1 mark)

Despite my good practice, there are still weaknesses in my performance due to nerves when performing in the arena. Sometimes, if my vaulting takes place first, I panic during my floorwork routine as the pressure is on me to score maximum points. Sometimes my timing coming out of the cartwheel is not consistent. (1 mark) Another weakness affecting my technique consistency is my mood; if I do not interpret the music well, my routine can look a bit rigid and my linking skills can look rushed. (1 mark)

TOP EXAM TIP

Exams are only one method of assessing your strengths and abilities, therefore try not to stress about the exam outcome. Relax and enjoy taking this opportunity to tell the examiner what you know.

Question 6

Choose an activity.

(a) Give a detailed description of a complex skill, outlining what makes it difficult to perform.

4

HINT This question is testing your knowledge about the different ways skills are classed or referred to. Try to include specific examples to support your answer. Remember, what one person finds difficult or complex another person may find easy.

In tennis, a complex skill I found difficult to perform was my cross court drive. The reason I found this so difficult was because of the demands of the execution phase of the shot. The precision required to play this shot is extremely high. In the preparation phase, I have to move early to the ball, take it high in front of me and transfer my body weight, rotating powerfully from the waist. (1 mark) My racket head speed must be extremely quick as I follow through across my body in the execution phase. I have to make sure that I disguise the shot but at the same time ensure my placement is tight to the sideline. (1 mark) This shot is played from mid or rear court. It can be played from both my forehand and backhand sides, the backhand being the harder of the two. Quick decisions and good footwork are essential. (1 mark)

Another difficulty in playing this shot is that if I fail to time it correctly and my angle of delivery is too shallow, then it restricts my ability to get back into position early enough to defend. (1 mark)

(b) Describe, in detail, the practice method(s) you used to develop this complex skill.

6

HINT The question is testing your acquired knowledge about relevant practice methods. There are many types that can be used; those given in the answer are just examples. Think about relevant practice methods you have used, and give as much detail as you can to access full marks.

When developing my cross court drive I decided to use repetition and combination drills to develop my technique and shot placement.

Repetition of the shot I felt was the quickest way to help me refine my technique, as I could get consistent feedback and accurate ball feeds from my partner who is the same standard as me.

I returned the ball twenty times, not worrying about placement or accuracy. I then repeated this drill, only this time I aimed at cones placed deep and near the sideline. (1 mark)

The nature of these drills helped me to make fine adjustments to improve my technique, mainly the timing in my follow-through and racket head angle. They also helped me to develop good footwork and anticipation. (1 mark)

The other advantage of these types of drills was that I could get my partner to vary the type of feed. By varying the height, speed and direction of the ball I made sure that I could adapt to game pressure.

(1 mark)

I then moved on to combination drills which resembled game pressure. Not only did these drills help me to execute the cross court drive more realistically, but I was able to develop other parts of my game such as fitness and mental focus. With my partner, we would start the rally with a serve always aimed at the left hand side, because it develops topspin, then continue with two to three line drives and, then, I would finish with a cross court drive. After this we would start the rally again. (1 mark)

Although I knew the sequence of the shots to be played, the nature of these drills allowed me to play a greater range of shots, so forced me to be accurate while refining my footwork and court coverage. (1 mark)

The last combination drill consisted of rallies being played randomly from side to side. This encouraged me to focus hard on good footwork, body positioning and alertness, and to play the cross court either from my forehand or backhand side. These drills forced me to deal with the challenges I would face when playing a competitive match. (1 mark)

(c) Discuss the principles you considered to ensure your practice was effective. Give examples of how these were used within your sessions.

6

HINT   The examples of how you applied principles of practice will depend on how you managed your practice sessions. Link these examples to the principles you applied to support your answer.

I knew I should consider a range of important factors to ensure success. The factors I considered were the type of practice that would suit me best, the partner who would feed me, the number of drills that I would include, the feedback I would get once my targets had been reached, rest periods and varying my drills. (1 mark)

Once I had selected the best type of practice for me, by which I mean the most enjoyable and motivating, I set realistic targets that I wanted to achieve. For example, in the repetition drills, the first twenty feeds I returned could be placed fairly accurately near the sideline, then, increasing the pressure, I had to aim at the cones to improve my angle and direction. (1 mark) I knew to take rest periods which helped me regain focus and assess my success rate. My partner and observation record sheet gave me the feedback necessary to progress. (1 mark)

At any stage I could increase the degree of difficulty to make me work harder: for example, in the combination rallies I could play a forehand cross court, get back to base and chase to the other side to play the more difficult backhand cross court drive. (1 mark)

By varying the combination drills, I was motivated to do well. My ability to read the game improved and I felt that I was more confident in returning from the baseline and creating more winning shots when using my cross court drive. (1 mark) I always monitored any improvements by looking at my recent match results and comparing how I performed against better players. Importantly, I knew kinaesthetically that my follow-through had a more 'whip' like action and so my shot delivery had much more power and spin in it. (1 mark)

(d) What are the benefits of using a model performer to help you to perform this complex skill?   4

HINT   There are many benefits of using a model performer when developing your performance. Try to highlight their special importance when developing a complex skill. Convince the examiner of this by offering relevant examples.

Watching model performers always helps improve your skill level. This is especially important when the skill is difficult such as the complex skill of a cross court drive. Model performers are at the top of their sport and their execution of groundstroke techniques is deadly. I regularly watch Andy Murray and Rafa Nadal for inspiration and aspire to be better than I am at the moment. (1 mark)

By watching video playback of their action I can learn more quickly about correct footwork, body positioning and preparation of the racket head. I can then try to put this into my own cross court drive action during my court practice. (1 mark) My playing partner is considered a model performer, which is excellent, as I can get accurate feeds and immediate external feedback about things that I am doing well and what I still need to do to improve. (1 mark) Playing against model performers makes me more determined to succeed. I have to be prepared to chase every ball and take any opportunity to get cross court drives in to stand any chance of getting points against them. (1 mark)

TOP EXAM TIP

If this is your last question, you will be glad. However, one final read over your answer may jog your memory, and you may still be able to add in extra information to offer more detail.

Worked answers to Practice Paper B, Area 4

STRUCTURES, STRATEGIES AND COMPOSITION

TOP EXAM TIP

Do not just open the exam paper and glance at the questions. Read the whole paper and answer the question you feel will gain you most marks first.

Question 7

Choose an activity.

(a)   Describe a structure, strategy or composition you have used in this activity. Briefly outline the role you played.   6

HINT   There are two parts to this question. Give as much detail as you can in the first part of the question as the second part is asking for a brief outline, so is worth fewer marks.

The activity I have selected is football and the structure we used was a 3-5-2 formation. This involved three defenders playing at the back with one defender covering the wide right area, another defender covering the middle area and the third defender covering the wide left area. (1 mark)

We had five midfield players. The two wide midfield players play wide near the touchline and can help out in attack or defence when required, giving us extra cover in defence or extra options when attacking. (1 mark)

The centre midfield player looks after the middle area of the park and the other two players in midfield have more of a free role to move up and down the park as required. (1 mark)

There are two strikers whose main jobs are to either hold the ball up if they receive long passes from defence or passes from midfield, or go for goals themselves if they receive the ball. They can also get into the box to get on the end of any crosses. (1 mark)

My role was that of the striker playing up front. I played on the left side, as I am left footed and feel comfortable on that side. I had to make myself available for passes from the midfield or run into space to receive long passes from the defence. (1 mark)

Another part of my play was to try to put some pressure on the opponents' defence and to force mistakes from them. I would try to close them down when they had the ball and force them into a bad pass or prevent a simple pass being made to one of their team. (1 mark)

(b) Explain the benefits that can be gained when applying your chosen structure, strategy or composition.

4

One of the benefits that this structure allows is the ability to support the two strikers. This can be done through the two wide wing backs supporting the attack by creating attacking options. They can play out wide and provide crosses into the box for the strikers to attack. (1 mark)

This can also be achieved through having one of the midfield players playing just behind the front two strikers. They can be available for a short pass, or to pass the ball to the strikers, and then get in behind the defence by making a penetrating run forward, thus allowing an attacking option. (1 mark)

Another benefit is that we can dominate midfield, as there are five players there. This means we can crowd the midfield with bodies, making it difficult for the opposition to pass the ball and keep possession, forcing errors or preventing passes reaching the forwards. (1 mark)

The final benefit it can provide is helping out in defence. One of the central three midfield players can sit in a holding role just in front of the back three defenders. They can be available to help in defence and be able to pick up short passes from the defence or clear the ball up to the strikers. (1 mark)

(c) (i) Explain **one** limitation that has to be taken into account when applying this structure, strategy or composition.

2

(ii) Explain what you would do to overcome this limitation.

2

(i) One limitation when applying the 3-5-2 strategy is that long balls played from the opponents' defence straight to their attackers can cause problems, as there are only three defenders back to cover. Gaps can be exploited and this could end up with the opposition forwards having chances to score goals. (1 mark)

This is likely to happen if we are playing against a team who are playing 4-2-4 and have four forwards against our three defenders. They are more likely to play long balls as they have an extra player in attack compared to our defence. (1 mark)

(ii) In order to overcome this limitation, there are some options that we could apply. First of all we could take one of our midfield five players and get them to drop back into defence and match up their attack by having four defenders against their four attackers. This means we could man mark each player and cut down scoring opportunities. (1 mark)

Another option we could use to overcome this limitation would be to change our defensive system and play a sweeper. We would change to a 4-2-4 defence, but one of the defenders would act as a sweeper and play behind the three defensive players. This player could defend any ball that went behind our defensive three and hopefully prevent goal scoring chances. (1 mark)

(d) Discuss some of the decisions you faced when performing in this structure, strategy or composition to ensure you carried out your role effectively.

6

As one of the strikers, I was often a target to receive a pass, whether it was a long pass from defence or a short pass from midfield. I had to look for space and time my run into that space to get away from my marker. Going too early could result in me being offside. (1 mark)

When I received a pass, I had to decide what I was going to do. Should I go straight for goal alone? Or hold the ball up for either midfielder to support me? Or link up with my fellow striker? (1 mark)

I had to decide how to effectively make space in attack. Would I come short to receive the ball and, with my back to goal, hold off the defender and shield the ball from them before laying the ball off to a team mate, or would I draw my defender away and create space for my fellow attacker to run in to receive the ball? (1 mark)

When I received the ball in a position near the goal, I had to decide where to place the shot on goal. I would look at the angle I was at, where the goalkeeper was positioned, and how far out I was from the goal before taking a shot. (1 mark)

Another decision that I was faced with was where to take up position when crosses were coming into the box from the wings. Beforehand it was agreed that, if the cross came from the left, I would attack the near post and my fellow striker would go to the back post and vice versa from the opposite side. (1 mark)

Finally, I had to think about defending. I had to time my run and put pressure on defenders when they had the ball, trying to force mistakes or prevent easy passes. Sometimes I even won the ball from them or forced them to play the ball back to the goalkeeper. (1 mark)

TOP EXAM TIP

It is better not to use bullet points in answers. Instead, use sentences to expand the points you want to highlight.

Question 8

Choose an activity and a structure, strategy or composition.

(a) Discuss why it is important to gather information on your performance when applying the structure, strategy or composition. Outline the strengths and weaknesses you found from the information gathered.

6

HINT   Think of ways in which you could gather information and justify why they would be important. Remember to briefly describe your strengths and weaknesses to access full marks in the question.

The activity that I have selected is basketball and the strategy is half court man-to-man defence. I gathered information on our strategy to find out our strengths and weaknesses. This allowed us to find out if the defence we were playing was effective and to identify which parts we were good at and what we were poor at. (1 mark)

This information was important because we could use it to plan a training programme which we could then carry out, hopefully leading to improvement in the long term. (1 mark)

We were also able to find out if any changes or adaptations were needed when we were applying the strategy. It allowed us to pinpoint particular parts that were really effective and that the opposition were finding hard to cope with. (1 mark)

Finally it allowed us to look closely at particular players when they were playing and see how they were coping with the opposition players they were asked to mark. We were also then able to pick out strengths and weaknesses of players in the opposition and perhaps use this to our advantage. (1 mark)

The strengths that we found were that we were good at picking the opposition players up when they crossed into our half and that we were always basket-side when marking them, which gave us a chance of keeping them away from our basket. (1 mark)

Our main weaknesses were that, if one of our defenders lost the player they were marking, we were poor as a team at playing help defence. This meant that the player from the opposition, who had got free, was often able to drive to the basket instead of one of our defenders getting across to mark them. We were also poor at moving our feet when defending. (1 mark)

(b) Describe the course of action you took to improve the weaknesses you identified in part (a).   4

HINT   The answer given below is only one course of action that you may have used. There may be other ways to achieve the same outcome.

We carried out particular drills to improve both weaknesses. To improve our footwork, we did a drill where a player stood in front of the class and we all faced him, staying in the correct defensive position. He would point which direction we should go and we would move, staying in the correct position all the time. Each time he pointed we would go a different way. (1 mark)

We also practised facing an opponent who had to dribble down the court slowly, changing direction as they wished. The defender had to stay between them and the basket and move their feet as they progressed down the court. When the teacher blew the whistle the attacker had to try to drive past and the defender had to try to stay with them or force an error from them. (1 mark)

To improve our help defence, we carried out a 5v5 shell defence drill. We set up a defence where we all took up either 'ball', 'deny' or 'help' defence, depending on who had the ball in attack. When the ball was passed to a particular player we all had to move to the correct position for the ball, deny or help defence. (1 mark) This allowed us to see who plays help defence depending on where the ball is in relation to the basket.

We then made this drill active and started playing 3v3 using the above principles. Then, we moved to 4v4 and eventually 5v5, so we could get used to all positions as well as concentrating on help defence. We did this initially half court, but on 5v5 we moved to play a full game using half court man-to-man defence. (1 mark)

(c) Having carried out a course of action to improve your weaknesses, how did you monitor the effectiveness of your training programme? Briefly outline what would be your future development needs having carried out your programme.

6

HINT
There are many ways to monitor your training programme. Below are examples of a couple of methods. Think of what **you** did.

We monitored the effectiveness of our defence by videoing a game against the same team that we played before. We also completed an observation schedule in conjunction with the video, giving us results of our performance using half court man-to-man. (1 mark)

The observation schedule was split up into columns which corresponded to each part of the half court man-to-man, for example stay between ball and basket, force opponent to make mistake, help in defence, etc. We looked at the video then filled in the observation schedule. (1 mark)

We filled in each section with a tick or cross, depending on whether we had been successful or not, and this gave us statistics on how effective our training programme had been. We were then able to compare these statistics with the data we had gathered when we played the same team previously. (1 mark)

Finally, we also received feedback from our teacher, on a regular basis, on how we were doing when playing man-to-man. He gave us advice on what to do if there was a problem or told us what was working well. Afterwards he would reflect on the performance compared to the previous game. (1 mark)

Having carried out our training programme, we will now try to work on our communication. While we have improved our help defence, we do not always let one another know when we require help. There are still occasions when the person who has lost their player has not shouted for help, resulting in us losing a basket. (1 mark)

Also, we would now like to look at being able to learn to double-team a player who is causing problems for us as a team. This would enable us to take away the opportunity for this player to score as many baskets.

(1 mark)

(d) Why is the monitoring process important?

4

HINT
This question is asking for acquired knowledge about why monitoring is important.

Monitoring is important because it provides information on our progress and it allows us to see if the training programme that we are working on is at the right intensity and is effective. (1 mark)

It also provides us with information on the specific aspects that the training programme is targeting and whether improvements are actually being made in that area or not. That means changes can be made if necessary.
(1 mark)

Monitoring also provides information that can be compared to previous data. From this we can find out if we have improved or not, and we can also get information on what may still need to be improved and worked on in the future. (1 mark)

Finally, monitoring can be a source of motivation if things are going well. This will give us the desire to keep working hard as we can see that we are improving our performance. (1 mark)

PERFORMANCE APPRECIATION

TOP EXAM TIP

Remember, exams are designed to reward your hard preparation and study. Relax and just simply recall what you know.

Question 1

Choose an activity.

(a)   When preparing for a **quality** performance, describe the various factors you took into account.   **4**

HINT   The content of your answer will depend on your performance experiences.

To be prepared for a quality performance in gymnastics a number of different factors must be in place. Firstly, my technical skills need to be up to scratch so that I can perform well in my floorwork routine and when vaulting. I need consistency in the basic skills and to be able, if I can, to apply more complex skills.   (1 mark)

I also need to be physically fit to cope with the demands of the floorwork routines. I must be able to show height in my tumbling combinations, which requires speed, power and good co-ordination.   (1 mark)

I must be mentally prepared so that I remain calm and focused. Good visualisation of the vault I am about to perform helps me to time my run up to the board. (1 mark) I need to have different strategies on the go so that if my first vault or routine does not go according to plan, I can change it or re-order it so that I get the best judge marks.   (1 mark)

(b)   Explain how you planned your performance development to ensure you were ready to produce your best possible **quality** performance.   **6**

HINT   This question requires both a brief description and an explanation of the training considerations.

I planned to cope more effectively by looking at my performance DVDs. From the DVDs, I was able, with the help of my coach, to detect which parts of my vault were not exact and where I lost most points. (1 mark) I then focused on refining specific technical errors and applied a whole-part-whole approach to my training. This involved performing my whole vault repeatedly and selecting the part that caused most problems. (1 mark) This was a specific way to develop a range of required fitness areas, namely my physical, technical and mental fitness, at the same time. The repetitive performances allowed me to take a longer drive up run to gain height, while improving my focus and timing. (1 mark) I felt that this was a challenging way to prepare for quality performances. I also included plyometric jumps in my drive runs to develop the explosive power I would need at take-off. (1 mark) I knew my main consideration was to take account of training principles and intensity. I have to perform at 100% intensity, which is tiring; therefore I had to take rest periods and alter my plyometric work rates. (1 mark) I ensured that my training sessions finished with competitive conditions. I performed my floorwork routine first, then my vaults, as this is the order in my compulsory performances. Improved power and faster drive gave me more peak height to rotate.   (1 mark)

(c) Discuss how individual differences can affect the outcome of a performance.

Outline a performance situation where your individual characteristics affected the outcome.   6

Everybody responds differently when participating in sport. Depending on their own specific characteristics, people will handle pressure differently and this can greatly affect performances. Some people are intrinsically motivated, while others are extrinsically motivated to do well.   (1 mark)

Personality traits are inherited and can determine how the performer handles their mood and outlook. Some love the pressure of the role they play, others hate competition.   (1 mark)

Personal characteristics, such as motivation, confidence, determination, being fearless, being a good leader, can affect not only the way skills are executed, but the performance of others in a team activity.   (1 mark)

Self belief in your ability can have a positive or negative impact on the outcome of your performance. For example, it can help you rise to the challenge when under pressure. If you get stuck, you can easily adapt or change what you are doing to make performance better.   (1 mark)

I am a self motivated person and have good self belief in my abilities as a gymnast. I perform on my own and so rely on my determination to succeed, as mistakes can be made if I do not concentrate. For competitions I have to select the order of my vaults. The more complex they are, the more marks I gain, so I always go for the most complex vaults.   (1 mark)

Once, during a competition, I was behind in my ranking. I made the decision to perform my most complex vault first. I knew that, if I nailed it, I would gain high marks from the judges. It was a risk, as the height of my rotation had to be spot on. Although nervous, I took a slightly longer run up and managed to land perfectly on my dismount. As a result, my confidence was high and I was able to complete my floorwork routine later on in the day with ease. I won the competition outright.   (1 mark)

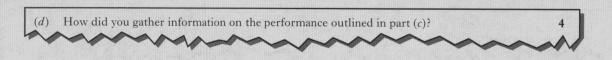

(d) How did you gather information on the performance outlined in part (c)?   4

During my gymnastic routines, I always gather information on my performance. The most reliable of all is video footage of my performance. It is this information, along with feedback received from my coach, that enables me to move up into the next category and do well. (1 mark) The video is extremely valid as it shows my live performances. A vault is only a few seconds long. Without this visual feedback I would not improve. The pause, rewind and split screen comparisons help me pinpoint my weaknesses. (1 mark) My coach discusses technical weaknesses and then burns my video performance with her commentary onto disc so that I can listen to it when practising on my own. (1 mark) I keep a record of marks gained in both my vault and floorwork routines for comparisons and to motivate me to do better. My record sheet contains judge certificates with progress marks and pointers for future improvements.   (1 mark)

Question 2

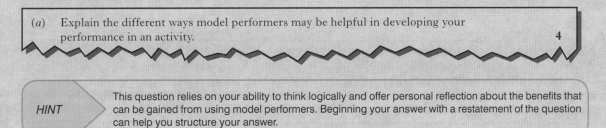

(a) Explain the different ways model performers may be helpful in developing your performance in an activity.

4

> **HINT** This question relies on your ability to think logically and offer personal reflection about the benefits that can be gained from using model performers. Beginning your answer with a restatement of the question can help you structure your answer.

There are many different ways model performers can be helpful in developing my performance.

For example, watching model performers can inspire me to achieve higher performance standards. By watching them I can get a visual picture of their effectiveness when performing and get different ideas on how to execute moves, skills or tactics. (1 mark)

I can copy them and set my performance targets. For example, during basketball practice sessions I use similar drills to those of the model performer and also work towards making my rebounding more consistent. (1 mark) Another benefit of the model performer is that I receive valuable feedback from them, as they can identify technique faults and offer constructive criticism about the best way to develop my technique. (1 mark) They can be a source of motivation by encouraging me to do well, which increases my confidence. (1 mark)

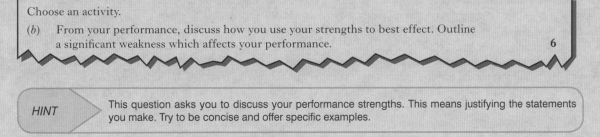

Choose an activity.

(b) From your performance, discuss how you use your strengths to best effect. Outline a significant weakness which affects your performance.

6

> **HINT** This question asks you to discuss your performance strengths. This means justifying the statements you make. Try to be concise and offer specific examples.

In basketball, I feel I have a wide range of strengths which makes me a threat when playing power forward. I have good physical fitness, especially cardio-respiratory endurance, which helps me work hard throughout the duration of the game. I have very good explosive power, allowing me to win many rebounds. This is a real advantage, especially if I miss my shot. (1 mark)

When defending, I mark very tightly and force my opponents into making mistakes. Being agile and having good timing and anticipation helps me make valuable steals and set up early offence options. (1 mark) My good agility also helps me to be balanced when making 'fake and go' moves. This lets me fool my opponent into thinking I am going one way when I am actually going the other way. (1 mark)

My technical skills are a real strength; when passing, dribbling and shooting I am usually very consistent and very much in control of what I am doing, leading to fewer mistakes being made. (1 mark)

I am a competitive player and do not like to lose. This is my downfall, as I get too aggressive and can get into foul trouble. Not controlling anxiety well is a fault of mine. (1 mark)

As team captain, I try really hard at all times. I feel I inspire the team as I rarely give up. I continually encourage them to keep going, especially if we are trailing by a few baskets. (1 mark)

(c) Discuss how you would plan your training to

    (i) improve your weakness

    OR

    (ii) maintain or further develop your strengths.

6

HINT — In your discussion, you need to highlight your thoughts about planning and justify your training method selection.

To maintain my fitness strengths, I, first of all, prioritised the strengths that I would concentrate on in my training. As my role involves a lot of court movement, I decided to focus on my cardio-respiratory endurance and agility. I decided to do extra fitness training outwith my normal team practice. Although at team training, we completed a lot of repetition drills, which helped my cardio-respiratory endurance, it was not enough for the level I play at. (1 mark)

I could have chosen a number of different methods, but decided interval training would be the most specific to maintain both my CRE and agility, as I included running and sprinting over various distances and altering rest periods.

(1 mark)

I trained three times a week and knew to consider the principles of training. I used a training record to monitor my route and timed results. This also kept me motivated to do well. (1 mark)

I knew to make sure I was in my training zone and borrowed a heart-rate monitor to make sure my results were accurate. My work periods had to be at least 20 minutes long. (1 mark)

I used the 18 yard box of my park football pitch as my training area. For the first three weeks. I ran at an even pace for ten minutes around the box and followed this with a five-minute stretching regime. I did this run continuously with no rest period. Immediately after stretching, I jogged the length of the box, turning quickly, which also developed my agility. I then sprinted down a zig-zag line and jogged back to the start to repeat. I then finished with a five-minute cool down to avoid strain. In total, I spent 20 minutes running. (1 mark)

I then overloaded by increasing my work rate. I increased the time to 30 minutes and upped the intensity of my running speed. In my zig-zag runs, I tried to sprint a wee bit faster and for variety included 2/3 jumps, pretending I was rebounding. This time, I did take a rest period after each repetition, as I was more tired after the sprints – I only took 15 seconds recovery. (1 mark)

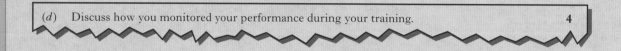

(d)   Discuss how you monitored your performance during your training.   4

I used a heart-rate monitor, kept a record sheet of my runs and noted down very briefly how I felt.

I linked the heart-rate monitor to my computer and got a graph print out. This showed, at a glance, the amount of time I was training in my zone and the amount of time I was training out of my zone. (1 mark)

The record sheet contained columns where I recorded the number of times I passed the start cone, which indicated whether I maintained my pace. This was simple and easy to complete and I could compare results on a daily basis. (1 mark)

On my record sheet (although not all the time) I noted down how I felt. This was important for the zig-zag sprinting because I hated it. It did get easier so I suppose it kept me motivated. (1 mark)

I knew that increasing targets and then comparing results was an accurate way of showing improvements. It also let me adapt my training. At team practice, I would race my team mate around cones to check whether I had got faster. (1 mark)

Worked answers to Practice Paper C, Area 2

PREPARATION OF THE BODY

Question 3

(a) • Physical fitness
• Skill-related fitness
• Mental fitness

Select **two** of the three types of fitness above and explain the importance of these two types when performing in an **individual** activity.

6

> HINT   Think about your own activity. Include two examples from each type of fitness to gain full marks.

The activity I have chosen is athletics, the event is the long jump and the first type of fitness I have chosen is physical fitness. Power is important in the long jump for an effective take-off. Power is a combination of strength and speed and each of these aspects is important in the phases of the long jump.   (1 mark)

Speed is very important in the run up phase of the jump. You want to reach maximum speed in your run up on the approach to the take-off board. By having maximum speed at take-off, more power will be generated. More speed will allow more momentum at take-off and will give you more height, resulting in more time in the air and leading to a greater distance being achieved.   (1 mark)

Power also requires strength. Directing explosive strength downwards onto the take-off board will result in more force pushing you upwards. This, combined with the speed from the run up, helps create the power to propel you forward into the pit to achieve a greater distance.   (1 mark)

The second type of fitness I have chosen is mental fitness.

Mental rehearsal is very important in the long jump. It allows you to focus on the jump ahead and rehearse the parts necessary for a good jump. You can imagine the jump ahead and go through the approach run, take-off and jump in your mind; this prepares you and increases your confidence.   (1 mark)

Managing emotions is important. It allows you to control your feelings and deal with pressure in difficult or competitive situations. In a competition you can block out spectators or your opponents by keeping calm and relaxed before you jump. This lowers anxiety and allows you to perform to a high standard.   (1 mark)

Level of arousal can also be important. This is the body's ability to respond to psychological changes as a result of increased adrenalin. If you have just achieved a big jump in a competition and taken the lead, you will be in a very positive frame of mind and this can often have a good effect on your performance.   (1 mark)

(b) • Physical fitness
• Skill-related fitness
• Mental fitness

From the three types of fitness above, select the **remaining** type of fitness, not chosen in part (a), and explain the importance of this type when performing in a **team** activity.

4

> HINT   Read this part of the question carefully. Remember, you are being asked to select the type of fitness you have not selected to answer in part (a).

The activity that I have chosen is hockey and I have chosen skill-related fitness. Agility is important in hockey as it allows you to keep tight control of the ball and to change direction quickly, which are necessary when you want to dribble past players or move into space to create an opportunity for a shot on goal.   (1 mark)

Reaction time is important for goalkeepers, in particular when they have to dive to save, stop a shot or move out quickly to narrow the angle when an attacker is moving towards goal.   (1 mark)

Co-ordination is important in hockey, as there are a series of movements, such as passing, dribbling and shooting, where you have to use different parts of the body at the same time. You must be able to carry out these movements smoothly and efficiently and having good co-ordination will allow this. (1 mark)

Timing is important when you want to tackle an opponent and try to win the ball from them. You have to reach in for the ball at the correct moment and try to flick it away or take it off them. Timing the movement will allow you to do this. (1 mark)

(c) Select **one** of the types of fitness from part (a) or part (b). Discuss what you took into account when you planned a fitness training programme for this type of fitness. Give examples from your programme to support your answer.

6

HINT   There are two parts to the question. The discussion part is the part you need to answer in more detail to gain marks.

I have selected physical fitness from part (a). First of all, I looked at the principles of training I would use when planning my training. The first one I made sure I used was specificity. I found out from data taken that power was a weakness when taking off, so I made sure that my training was going to be specific to that weakness. It also had to be specific to my performance improvement. (1 mark)

I decided on an eight-week training programme and that I would train three times per week, on every second day to allow my body to rest. I trained by doing plyometrics as well as practising my speed and specific jump practices. (1 mark)

In my plyometric training, I did a series of exercises specifically designed to improve the power needed for the take-off. These were jumping and bounding exercises such as single leg jumps, speed bounds and leg hops. I did two sets of each exercise with 45 seconds rest in between. (1 mark)

My sprint training consisted of short sprints of 20/30 metres doing three sets of each. I also worked on long jump exercises which were specifically based on sprinting, leg power and take-off. (1 mark)

I also took into account progression and overload as my training progressed and my power and strength increased. I could increase the number of sets that I completed and reduce the recovery time between each set or I could train for another session per week. (1 mark)

Finally, I took into account how I would monitor my training. I decided to keep a training diary, writing down my programme and making notes on how I felt after each session. It also allowed me to keep a note of any changes that were made to my programme. (1 mark)

(d) Describe **one** method you used to monitor the effectiveness of your training programme. Explain why this method was appropriate.

4

HINT   Refer only to one method you have used in class. Do not answer on all the methods you may have used; give as much detail as you can on the method you choose to describe.

I decided to monitor my training programme by keeping a diary, recording information about my training as well as my actual results from jumps that I had made. After each training session I wrote down information on how I felt and what I had carried out in that session. (1 mark)

This allowed me to monitor and record information on my performance so I could then judge the effectiveness of my programme. It allowed me to see whether I had made progress and also when I needed to change the intensity of my training. (1 mark)

I also kept a record of my results from training as well as in actual competitions. This gave me the opportunity to reflect on whether my training programme was benefiting my whole performance and also allowed me to compare previous results and keep a permanent record of my performances in actual competitions. (1 mark)

Finally, by keeping a diary I was able to see if my short and long term goals had been achieved. If I had achieved my short term goals, it motivated me to then achieve my long term goals. (1 mark)

Question 4

(a)   Select **two** different activities. Describe two physical fitness requirements that are
similar in both activities. Give examples to support your answer.

4

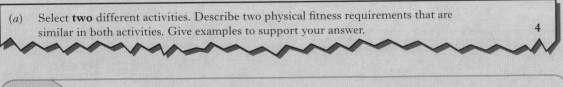

HINT   Read the question carefully. Remember, you are being asked to select two aspects of physical fitness.
Giving relevant examples related to the chosen aspects will enhance your answer.

The two activities I have chosen are volleyball and gymnastics. The first aspect of physical fitness which is used
in both is strength. In volleyball, I need good strength in my legs when jumping to spike the ball if my team
is attacking and to block when the opposition is attacking using a spike. (1 mark) In gymnastics, strength is
important in the arms and shoulders when I am performing a handstand. I must have good strength in my arms
and shoulders to be able to hold my bodyweight on my hands.   (1 mark)

The second aspect that is similar in both activities is power. Power is required in volleyball to spike the ball
downwards fast and hard into the opponents' court after the ball has been set up by my team. (1 mark) Power is
also required in gymnastics when performing moves such as a handspring, where you need power to push off the
ground from your hands and propel your body in a forward motion to land on your feet.   (1 mark)

(b)   Select **one** of the activities described in part (a) and explain why skill-related fitness
is important when performing.

4

HINT   Read this part of the question carefully. Remember, you are being asked to explain. A good way of
answering is to describe aspects of skill-related fitness and then give reasons why they are important.

The activity I have selected is volleyball. Agility is important in volleyball, as players have to move quickly to get
into position on the court to be able to play a dig from a service. This may involve players changing direction to
get into a low position to return the ball.   (1 mark)

Having good agility allows players, first of all, to reach the ball when it is played to different parts of the court
and then to recover quickly back into position once a player has played a return ball.   (1 mark)

Timing is also important in volleyball. When a spiker is going to spike the ball, they must be able to run into
position, take off and jump high and then be able to strike the ball downwards fast and hard into the opponents'
court. In order to achieve this, the timing of the run and take-off are crucial so that the spiker is in the correct
position in the air to execute the spike effectively.   (1 mark)

Finally, co-ordination is important. For example, when serving, a player has to throw the ball in the air and
be able to strike the ball overhead to get it over the net into the opponents' court. Players must have good
co-ordination to throw, watch and strike the ball.   (1 mark)

(c)   From the **other** activity selected in part (a), discuss why mental fitness is important.
Give examples to support your answer.

6

HINT   Remember, discussion requires you to offer opinion and justify how mental fitness is important to your
whole performance. For full marks you also need to give relevant examples of where mental fitness is
important.

When competing in a gymnastics competition, it is important to be able to manage your emotions. If there are
spectators at the event, you can become nervous and anxious. This can hinder your performance so it is crucial to
be able to block out distractions and focus fully on your performance.   (1 mark)

The crowd may be encouraging other competitors, or there may be other events taking place in the arena at the same time, so it is important that the gymnast remains fully focused on their performance and is not distracted by noise, etc.

(1 mark)

Mental rehearsal is also important. This is when the gymnast rehearses in their mind the action or routine they are going to perform. For example, it may be the floor routine and the sequence of moves they will carry out.

(1 mark)

The purpose of this is to rehearse in their mind the moves in the routine that flow together, as if they were actually doing them and executing them perfectly. This means the gymnast is fully focused on the task in hand. This can also speed up the learning process.

(1 mark)

Arousal can also affect gymnasts. The stress of competing can lead to increased heart rate, nervousness and being insecure which, in turn, will lead to a poor performance. So, it is important that the gymnast is at their optimal level of arousal, where they are able to cope with all the symptoms mentioned and be mentally ready to perform to their best ability.

(1 mark)

Finally, confidence and determination are important. When performing a particularly difficult vault, it is important to be confident in your ability to carry out the vault as well as possible. Lack of confidence will lead to mistakes and a lower score being achieved. Also, being determined will lead to full effort being made and could lead to a better execution of the vault, as the gymnast will want to do as well as possible.

(1 mark)

(d)   Select **one** of the aspects of fitness from your answers above. Select one method of training you used to develop this aspect. Explain why this method was appropriate. Describe, in detail, **one** training session using this method.

6

HINT   Remember, there are two parts to this question. The second part is linked to the first part. The second part is asking about one training session so think back to a lesson in class and describe what you did on that day.

I have selected volleyball and strength. The method of training that I have selected is conditioning. By using this method, I am able to improve not only strength but other aspects of fitness that will improve my performance in the game, such as agility, power, flexibility and co-ordination.

(1 mark)

This method also allows me to practise and improve the skills and movement required in the game at the same time, such as setting, spiking and service reception.

(1 mark)

Finally, training within the activity is easily set up, requires no specialist equipment and can be fun and enjoyable. This will motivate me, as I can train on the actual volleyball court and can practise and play by re-creating the fitness demands of a competitive game.

(1 mark)

In one training session, to improve my strength, I carried out a circuit on the court involving a set of exercises and game-related drills.

First of all, I started with a warm up, where I did some jogging and general stretching to get myself ready for my circuit ahead. The circuit was based on a group of exercises designed specifically to improve strength. I did 3 sets of each exercise, each lasting for 30 seconds, with a 45 second rest between each set.

(1 mark)

The exercises I carried out were: press ups and pull ups to improve strength in the arms and shoulders, squat jumps, stride jumps and wall jumps to improve the strength in my legs and, finally, walking lunges to strengthen my lower body because of the running and jumping involved in volleyball.

(1 mark)

Finally, I carried out some specific drills such as spiking and blocking drills, which are good for improving strength in the legs and arms. The drills included self bounce and hit practice, self throw and hit practise and repetition practice of setting and spiking and blocking. Each drill consisted of 10 reps working individually as well as in twos and threes. I did 3 sets of each drill. I then played in small games of 3v3, where I had to receive serve then dig and spike.

(1 mark)

Worked answers to Practice Paper C, Area 3

SKILLS AND TECHNIQUES

TOP EXAM TIP

Make sure you read the whole question before you begin. Double check that you can answer all four parts of the question and so could gain the full 20 marks. Good luck!

Question 5

(a) From an activity of your choice, outline some of the features of performance that can be identified at each of the stages of skill learning. Explain what you understand about each stage.

6

HINT The question is asking for your acquired knowledge and understanding. By outlining each of the stages based on an activity you have experienced, you will show the examiner you have a sound grasp of skill learning.

In football, players can be at one of the three stages of learning. At the cognitive stage, players do not fully understand how skills/techniques should be performed. Basic skills such as passing and dribbling are quite inconsistent and are often only just recognisable. (1 mark) Movement patterns are clumsy and players need to be reminded to look up when passing. They rely on lots of external feedback about how to improve. (1 mark)

At the associative stage, players usually have a good understanding of how skills/techniques should be performed. They are starting to make better decisions and can co-operate with their teammates more. (1 mark) Players have a better understanding of their role and, when using skills such as passing, dribbling and tackling, they look much more controlled. They also need less external feedback at this stage. (1 mark)

When players reach the autonomous stage, they have a very clear understanding of how skills/techniques are performed and when best they should be used to wrong-foot opponents and create options. Players rely on their own kinaesthetic feedback and can correct any errors almost immediately. (1 mark) They have a wide range of skills that are used effortlessly and with control and precision. Decision making is excellent when carrying out role-related duties and they display good co-operation abilities and work to the team's game plan. (1 mark)

(b) Select a skill or technique from your activity. Give a detailed analysis of your performance that shows your current stage of learning.

4

HINT Remember, your own stage of skill learning may be different from the one described in this answer. This is just one example. You are required to demonstrate your critical thinking by linking your stage to a specific skill/technique; in the example given – the ability to score in football.

When playing striker in football, I think that I am at the automatic stage of performance. Firstly, I represent my school team and play in tight matches most weeks and I perform consistently. In my position, I am expected to score goals. My tally for this is quite high and I can score well with my right foot and accurately with my head. (1 mark) I have a good ability on the ball. I am controlled and link up easily with my twin striker. I can anticipate moves and accurately receive passes to create goal-scoring opportunities. (1 mark) When under pressure from defenders, I can hold them off, using good balance and body weight to push them back allowing me turning room to get my shot off on target. (1 mark) If I miss, I have the ability to hustle in against defenders and rush towards the goal to take any ball parried by the keeper. Although I do not have a lot of time to shoot, I believe that I can accurately place the ball into the corners to avoid it being saved. (1 mark)

(c) When developing this skill or technique, discuss how you used your knowledge of skill learning to design an appropriate programme of work.

6

HINT Often a good way to start your answer is to begin with the question statement. This helps you to focus your thoughts and gives your answer structure.

My knowledge of skill learning helped me select the most appropriate types of drills to include in my programme of work. I understand that learning the skill of shooting happens when the appropriate drills are selected to show progression. (1 mark)

An appropriate programme had to be planned with drills designed to develop ball control and use of shooting opportunities. Scoring is an 'open skill' and I knew that my drills would need to be worked on in game-like scenarios. (1 mark) The purpose of the drills had to be clear and targets had to be set to show my improvements: for example, a set of corner kicks, ten being played into the box from right and left. I received the ball firstly without the defenders to allow me time on the ball. At the back of the goal was a target board which showed where my shot was being targeted. (1 mark) After some feedback from fellow strikers we removed target boards and did ten more repeats, this time adding in defenders to make it more challenging. (1 mark) Goal scoring is a combined skill of keeping the ball under control, pulling it out of the pathway of defenders and then making a lay off pass or taking the shot myself. Therefore, I had to be motivated to do well and try hard, even if at first I did not succeed. (1 mark) Once targets had been reached, I knew to observe my whole game performance to see if my goal scoring abilities were improving. At first, we played 7v7 before finishing with a full game. Any attempts made were recorded and compared against previous results. (1 mark)

> (d) Describe how you evaluated the effectiveness of the programme you used.   **4**

On completion of my practice programme I evaluated how effective it was by comparing my game performance and percentage shooting rate. During my drill training, a record sheet of on target, hit the cross bar and missed shots was completed. On the same sheet it was noted whether I had hit the ball with my feet or head. (1 mark) Two record sheets were used, one to record success rate with the target board and no defenders, the other to record repetition deliveries of corner kicks. These were then used to make comparisons. (1 mark) When playing matches, a match analysis sheet was completed. This was time-related and columned in sections of five minutes' game time. It was also more detailed and showed from where on the pitch I took the shot, how many attempts were made (especially at corners) and how many goals were scored, etc. (1 mark) As well as this supportive data, I also relied on my own opinion about the improvements I made in terms of accurate shots against number of attempts made and whether or not I had reached my personal short term targets. This let me judge whether my programme had been set at the correct level for me. (1 mark)

TOP EXAM TIP

Do not be put off when others in the exam hall leave before you. You will know your own write-up time – stick with this plan and do not rush.

Question 6

> Choose an activity and a skill or technique.
>
> (a) Describe how you gathered information on your performance in the selected skill or technique.   **4**

TOP EXAM TIP

After you read a question make quick bullet points about the important information you intend putting in your answer. If you run out of time, this will give the examiner an idea of your understanding of the topic being tested.

HINT > The question requires you to give an account of what you did. As you describe the steps taken, there should be a clear and logical link to the purpose and the relevance of the data collection methods used.

I decided to gather information about the quality of my trampoline sequence so that I could identify any problems with it and refine the more complex technique of my barani with full twist into forward open somersault. I used a combination of quality sheet and a video. This self evaluation report required me to answer questions after studying a video of my performance. (1 mark)

This showed my technical application of this complex technique. I was able to comment and get feedback on how effective I looked in the air, and also how I used tempo, direction, height and posture to get high artistic points. (1 mark)

I performed my sequence several times and had it videoed from two different heights. One video was taken at trampoline level and the other from a viewing gallery above. This made my analysis easier to complete and more accurate. (1 mark)

I was then able to compare my performance against model performers in my group and get valuable feedback on how effective my barani and somersault looked in comparison. This information then helped me plan my practice programme. (1 mark)

(b) Describe, in detail, a practice programme you used to develop this skill or technique. **6**

The barani and open front somersault is a complex and dangerous technique. Basically I need to be at maximum height with good balance to ensure good rotation and secondary height into the front open somersault. I decided to use a gradual build up approach in my practice programme. I also did some circuits to develop my power and flexibility. (1 mark)

I used gradual build up by isolating each technique of barani and open front somersault. I would then take into account work and rest periods. Rest periods are essential in trampolining to ensure the quality of my moves does not deteriorate. (1 mark) After my preparatory bounces, I performed one barani, then put a safety mat in to prevent injury. I did this several times, getting feedback mostly on my height but also the timing of the rotation. (1 mark) I did the same practice repeats for my open somersault, although I found I was able to progress more quickly with this technique and rarely needed the use of the safety mat. I then analysed my techniques using video playback, before doing several repeats of the combined actions. (1 mark) Once confident, I practised the combined actions again with the safety mat, removing it once my timing was perfect. Each session ended with me completing my whole 20 bounce sequence. (1 mark) To improve my posture and shape while in the air, part of my practice involved performing a short circuit routine aimed at improving my power and flexibility. I did 15 hops over mini hurdles and 20-second sustained stretches in three different positions. These were performed at 100% intensity. To ensure improvement, I increased the duration of my circuit. (1 mark)

(c) Outline what you understand about the following **three factors** when practising or refining skills and/or techniques.

- **motivation**
- **concentration**
- **feedback**
6

HINT The question is examining your acquired knowledge about the three influential factors that are important in skill learning and development. By offering two main points per factor you will demonstrate to the examiner your depth of understanding.

For successful and effective skill development, I know that the three factors of motivation, concentration and feedback are essential. Quite often they overlap and rely on one other.

Firstly, a performer needs to be motivated to do well. Sometimes success is not immediate and mistakes can be made. Self motivation encourages the performer not to give up. (1 mark) Performers need to be motivated to complete the full practice programme and be willing to work hard, otherwise their performance targets will not be met. (1 mark)

Concentration is definitely needed to ensure the performer remains focused on the task. The performer needs to listen to any instruction offered and try to fix any weaknesses in their skill or technique. (1 mark) Concentration is also required when putting the whole skill together, when combining one skill with another or when applying the skill in a game. This prevents errors from occuring. (1 mark)

Feedback can come from internal or external sources. It can be verbal, written or shown to the performer, and is best given immediately after the performer has tried the skill or technique. Provided the performer is willing to act upon the feedback, this will improve their performance. (1 mark) Feedback helps eliminate errors and helps the performer become more experienced in the skill or technique. It also increases motivation and confidence. (1 mark)

(d) Explain why it is important to monitor and review the effectiveness of your practice programme. **4**

HINT The question is examining your acquired knowledge about the purpose of monitoring. Make sure you include examples to convince the examiner of your depth of understanding.

Monitoring is very important and should be happening during all my practice sessions. As I practised, I knew to check on how I was progressing. I found that this kept me motivated and it provided me with immediate feedback. (1 mark)

It also allowed me to target the things I could still improve upon. If I found I was not reaching my performance targets, I could adjust them. Monitoring also let me see how I was doing compared to my classmates. It was a constant process and internally I could feel the improvements I was making but could also feel when I needed to work harder. (1 mark)

Reviewing my performance happened at the end, when I had completed my practice sessions. This let me compare my first performance to my most current standard. I could check if the practice programme had worked and also find out if I had reached my long term goals. Was I able to perform barani into open forward somersault better, not only when practising but during competition? (1 mark)

Reviewing my practice regime let me judge whether or not to continue with the same practice methods, focusing on the same techniques, or whether to move on and address another weakness. Reviewing was also an important source of motivation as I could set new personal goals for the future. (1 mark)

TOP EXAM TIP

Taking a few sips of water at the start and end of each question will help you to remain focused. Combine this with deep breathing and you should feel your knowledge rush into your mind. Relax and be confident.

Worked answers to Practice Paper C, Area 4

STRUCTURES, STRATEGIES AND COMPOSITION

Question 7

Choose an activity and a structure, strategy or composition.

(a) Discuss the strengths that players need to carry out this structure, strategy or composition effectively.

4

HINT In this question the strengths could refer to you as a player, as well as all the different positions that there are in your activity.

The activity I have selected is hockey. The strategy chosen is the penalty corner. An effective penalty corner requires good team work, so that every person carrying out a role knows exactly what their job is. Without a well-rehearsed corner, if one person doesn't fulfil their role or if a mistake is made, the execution of the corner will break down and the chance to score a goal will be lost. (1 mark)

As this strategy is a pre-planned routine, the attackers have an advantage, as they know what is going to happen whereas the defence can only guess. Players in particular roles must have a high level of skill. The strategy usually involves three fundamental passing skills: using a push pass accurately, stopping the ball cleanly and striking the ball powerfully towards goal. (1 mark)

Players must have good communication skills to make the corner effective: for example, using verbal codes so that each player knows what particular corner routine is to be carried out. They may also use hand signals as a code. A breakdown in communication will lead to a less effective corner being carried out as more mistakes are likely to be made. (1 mark)

Finally, players need to be mentally alert all the time. They need to fully focus and concentrate on their role in the strategy so they execute their part and ensure it is a success. (1 mark)

(b) Describe the problem(s) you faced when carrying out this structure, strategy or composition. Explain the effect it had on your performance.

6

HINT In this question you can refer, if you wish, to only **one** problem you faced. If you do, remember you will need to give much more detail than if you describe a few problems. This will also have a knock-on effect on the second part of the answer.

The first problem we had was that the first pass, from the person carrying out the corner to the person stopping the ball, was too slow and was often not accurate enough. It frequently went to the side of the stopper who had to readjust their position to stop the ball.   (1 mark)

This resulted in the whole play being slowed down and allowed the defence time to react quickly and run out to the person stopping the ball. This resulted in this player failing to stop the ball cleanly or being rushed to make a pass to the person who was to shoot towards goal.   (1 mark)

The next problem we had was that our two strikers who shot at goal often lacked the timing and power in the shot to score a goal. Too often, the shot at goal was blocked, saved or it missed, as it lacked power and accuracy. This was because the shot was weak and often wide of the goal.   (1 mark)

This resulted in many goal-scoring opportunities being wasted and a lack of success when gaining a penalty corner. The strikers also became less confident in carrying out their role as they were unable to score a goal. Often they would try to make another pass rather than score themselves.   (1 mark)

Finally, our strategy was too predictable, as we only had two types of corner that we felt comfortable with carrying out. Our strategy was either for one striker to be ready to strike the ball as soon as the ball was stopped, or for the person stopping the ball to play a square pass for the other striker to shoot.   (1 mark)

The defence was able to predict which strategy we were going to use and were able to close the play down early, as they knew where and to whom the ball was going to be passed. This resulted in quick pressure being applied and mistakes being made in our team.   (1 mark)

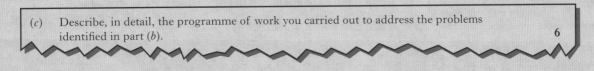

(c)   Describe, in detail, the programme of work you carried out to address the problems identified in part (b).   **6**

> **HINT**   In your answer give as much detail as possible about the practices you used to address the problems. You may well have used many practices so refer to them all to access full marks.

In order to address the problems, we, first of all, looked at improving the specific parts of the penalty corner which were letting us down, i.e. the push pass and the hitting. The person taking the corner worked with the stopper at improving the accuracy and speed of the pass. This was done in isolation, by using repetition practice, then moving on to practising using the 'D'.   (1 mark)

The two strikers worked together at practising their shooting from just inside the 'D', with a goalkeeper in position. If the keeper had managed to save the ball, they also worked on following the shot in and hopefully scoring on the rebound. This again was done in isolation.   (1 mark)

When each player had improved the specific skills needed for the penalty corner, we went back and practised the whole sequence to ensure all the parts could be linked together. We carried this out at normal game-like speed and with only a goalkeeper as opposition.   (1 mark)

Once this worked and we felt more confident, we increased the difficulty by having defenders in place. At first, the defenders ran out slowly to put a little pressure on us and then, after a few practices like this, they ran out at game-like pace so we were able to simulate the pressure of a live game.   (1 mark)

To get over the problem of the penalty corner being predictable, we practised different options we could use in a game to try to outmanoeuvre the opposition. We did this by walking through the option that we were going to use. We also decided to use particular codes for each option by calling out a particular word.   (1 mark)

Once we were familiar with all the options, we again practised them as before, with semi-active and then fully active defenders. This allowed us to use them in pressure situations and also allowed us to use our codes to see if they were effective in a game situation.   (1 mark)

(d)   Describe **one** method you used to see if your programme of work was effective. Explain why this method was appropriate.   **4**

> **HINT**   Read this part carefully. This question is asking for only one method. Make sure that you are able not only to describe that method, but also to explain why it was appropriate.

We evaluated our programme of work by videoing the next game that we played. This was carried out by our teacher, filming from the side of the pitch and was done each time we were awarded a penalty corner. This gave us evidence of how successful the corner was.   (1 mark)

In conjunction with the video, we used an observation schedule with all the parts of the penalty corner listed, such as accuracy of pass, clean stop and shot on target. We would tick or cross each part depending on whether it was carried out successfully or not. This was done later, after the game. (1 mark)

This method was appropriate because it gave us information from an actual live game. We could then break the penalty corner down into each part to see if improvements had been made. This meant we could also compare with previous results. (1 mark)

We could also replay and slow down the movements on video to look closely at each player and specific parts of the corner. This provided evidence about whether the training had been effective and allowed us to identify any further improvements that we needed to work on. (1 mark)

Question 8

Choose an activity.

(a) Describe a structure, strategy or composition you would usually select as your first choice. Explain why you would choose to use this structure, strategy or composition. **6**

> **HINT** Select a structure, strategy or composition that you can describe and offer explanations to show why you used it when performing.

The activity chosen is basketball. The structure chosen is a 2-1-2 zone defence. The 2-1-2 zone is a defensive structure where each player has responsibility for part of the key area close to the basket they are defending, rather than marking a particular player. The whole zone moves as a unit towards where the ball is being passed. (1 mark)

The zone has two players at the back of the zone, one defending each side. They are normally tall, and with the help of the centre, who is the player in the middle, they form a rebound triangle where they try to box out the attackers to gain possession of the ball on a rebound. (1 mark)

The two players at the front of the key are usually small and agile. Their job is to put pressure on the forwards of the opposing team when they are passing. They move very quickly towards the ball and can also try to intercept passes and start an attack. (1 mark)

The reason that we used the zone was to stop a team that had individual players who were very good at driving to the basket and scoring lay ups, as our individual defence was poor. The zone would prevent this, as there would be somebody in the space if a player tried to drive to the basket. (1 mark)

The zone was also used when we came up against a team who were good at screening one another and cutting to the basket when they attacked. The player being screened often lost their marker, allowing that player a clear run to the basket. (1 mark)

We also used the zone if we knew the team that we were playing had poor outside shooters. As the players from the attack could not penetrate the zone, they were forced to shoot from outside the key. If they missed we had a strong rebound triangle and could often regain possession of the ball. (1 mark)

(b) Describe an alternative structure, strategy or composition you might use in your chosen activity. **4**

> **HINT** This must be a different structure, strategy or composition to the one chosen in part (a). It also must be within the same activity, so make sure it is relevant.

The alternative structure that we used was a box-and-one zone. This is where four players take up positions with two at the front of the zone and two at the back of the zone. The fifth player was outside the zone, where their job was to put pressure on a particular player who was the only opposition player that was good at outside shooting. (1 mark)

This is similar to the outside player playing man-to-man as they are preventing the opposition player from scoring and being a threat to the basket. It puts great pressure on the attacking player and can also unsettle the rest of the attackers as their best player can be prevented from scoring, forcing them to shoot instead. (1 mark)

vThe zone has a gap in the middle so all the remaining four players have a slightly bigger area to cover. It is important they play as a unit and, when the ball comes into the middle, that they close it down quickly to prevent the other team having an easy shot at the basket. (1 mark)

Finally, at the front of the zone, the player who is the single player, can often gain possession of the ball and can start an attack quickly. The opposition will not have many defenders back as they will be round the key attacking, so often the front player can have an unopposed road to the basket. (1 mark)

(c) Choose **one** of the factors listed below:
- dealing with pressure
- being creative
- exercising effective solutions
- being perceptive.

Discuss how an awareness of this factor helped you to make decisions when applying your structure, strategy or composition selected in part (a). 6

HINT | This question is asking you to choose one factor. Look carefully at each before deciding on the one which you feel you can discuss the best in relation to your structure, strategy or composition. Remember, it must be the one selected in part (a).

I have selected dealing with pressure. When playing games, at first, we were poor at defending, as our two front guards were not putting enough pressure on the opposing forwards who were managing to score long range shots. Also, our two forwards were playing too far back in the key, instead of being out front at the top of the key. (1 mark)

Our teacher emphasised that any shot taken by the opposition should be pressurised whether it was successful or not. We went back into practice situations and worked on this. We played small-sided games of 2v1 where the single defender had to hassle the two attackers and try to block shots. This made us aware of the importance of pressuring the ball. (1 mark)

We then moved on to 3v2, where we had better success as two defenders could now try to block. From there, we moved on to full 5v5 practice games where we played half court, in which the priority was to prevent as many shots as possible from being taken without pressure being applied. (1 mark)

This allowed us to turn the situation round. Whereas before we were a team under pressure from long range shooters because of our poor defending, the pressure was now reversed and was on the attacking team, as we were closing their shots down quickly and putting them under pressure. (1 mark)

We could see that we were working better as a unit and, although there was the odd occasion when a shot would go in, we knew that, because we had practised putting pressure on the opposition, we had stopped losing easy baskets. Now the opposition had to work hard to break down our defence and score a basket. (1 mark)

Finally, our confidence grew as we were losing fewer baskets and stood a better chance of winning the game. Often we would force the opposition into making errors or force them to shoot from far out, and as we had a strong rebounding triangle, we were able to regain possession of the ball. (1 mark)

(d) Describe how you would evaluate the effectiveness of your structure, strategy or composition in relation to the factor selected in part (c). 4

HINT | Select methods you have used during your practical sessions. This will help you to describe the detail and highlight reliability and validity issues.

We evaluated our success by using a video camera to record our performance in games and also in practice. Our teacher would use the freeze-frame facility to show us where we were going wrong and point out the position of the defenders in relation to the ball. This would highlight our problems regarding putting pressure on the attackers. (1 mark)

In games, after carrying out our training programme, we did the same and were able to compare our performances with previous games. This highlighted whether we had improved and, again, we were able to see when we were applying pressure in games.

(1 mark)

We also used knowledge of our results. By using the video of games in conjunction with an observation schedule, we were able to see how many baskets we were losing from particular areas of the court and why this was happening. We had columns on the sheet with different criteria that should be applied when using zone defence.

(1 mark)

Finally, we also evaluated success by getting feedback from our teacher both during practice sessions and after games. He would give us verbal feedback on how we were doing and also gave us statistics on the number of shots successfully taken by the opposition in actual games. This let us know how we were doing and also gave us confidence if we were performing well.

(1 mark)